THE
CORPORATE
COUNSEL
SURVIVAL GUIDE

THE
CORPORATE
COUNSEL
SURVIVAL GUIDE

William E. Kruse

TORT TRIAL & INSURANCE PRACTICE SECTION

Cover design by Jill Tedhams /ABA Design

21 20 19 18 17   5 4 3 2 1

Library of Congress Cataloging-in-Publication Data

Names: Kruse, William E., author.
Title: The corporate counsel survival guide / William E. Kruse.
Description: Chicago : American Bar Association, 2017. | Includes index.
Identifiers: LCCN 2017018269| ISBN 9781634258869 | ISBN 163425886X
Subjects: LCSH: Corporate lawyers—United States.
Classification: LCC KF299.I5 K78 2017 | DDC 346.73/066023—dc23 LC record
    available at https://lccn.loc.gov/2017018269

Contents

About the Author

William Kruse, Gallup's Regulatory Compliance Officer and in-house legal counsel, works primarily with Gallup's government clients in the United States and around the world. He is also a board member of Gallup's government contracting subsidiary and the legal advisor to Gallup's Institutional Review Board. He is a litigation and regulatory compliance attorney with nine years of experience in US acquisition regulations, contracting, and procurement.

Prior to joining Gallup's legal team, Mr. Kruse worked for a litigation firm based in St. Louis, Missouri, where he handled railroad and maritime disputes as well as multidistrict litigation involving toxic torts.

Mr. Kruse is a member of the American Bar Association (ABA) and has served as chair of the Tort Trial and Insurance Practice Section (TIPS) Corporate Counsel Committee. He is also a member of the ABA TIPS Corporate Counsel Outreach Task Force and of the ABA TIPS Committee on Outreach to Young Lawyers.

Mr. Kruse is the author of several articles published in legal and business publications, including the *International In-House Counsel Journal* and *Ethikos*. He has presented at legal and business conferences, meetings, teleconferences, and webinars on a range of topics including procurement, white-collar and corporate crime, ethics and compliance, and business codes of conduct.

Mr. Kruse received his bachelor's degree in business from the University of Missouri–St. Louis and his juris doctorate from Florida International University. He attended law school while serving on active duty in the US Coast Guard, graduating seventh in his class.

Foreword

Making the decision to pursue an in-house counsel position can be daunting for a law firm attorney, in part because in-house positions can be so very different from working in a firm and can vary in meaningful ways from company to company. Having a guide such as this book when I was considering the transition from law firm to an in-house position, as well as when I was first starting my in-house position, would have been immensely helpful. While I read many blog posts and articles about in-house positions during my job search, I found that I had not fully anticipated the differences between practicing law in a law firm and as an in-house counsel. Both types of positions are rewarding in their personal and professional challenges and opportunities, but the differences can be quite significant and take some time to get used to after a transition from a law firm to in-house position.

Attorneys considering a jump to an in-house position are best served by doing as much research as possible on the nature of in-house counsel positions within the particular industries and companies for which they are interested in working. This book offers helpful insight into the unique aspects of serving as in-house counsel and provides a good foundation for those seeking to learn more about in-house counsel life. Because it is always better to go into a job search or a new job as prepared as possible, those who are considering an in-house counsel position will benefit from reading this book.

J. Catherine Kunz
Senior Counsel of Intelligence, Information, and Services
Raytheon Company

Preface

I can't thank the ABA enough for actually publishing this book. I wanted to write a book that was fun to read, passed on valuable advice for new in-house counsel, and wouldn't bore anyone to death in the process. I was personally shocked that anyone found my idea for writing this book to be worthy, and more shocked that my writing made it past the distinguished editors.

I owe two people more than anyone acknowledgment for making this book happen. One is my amazing boss, Steve O'Brien, who through his own book publishing inspired me to write as well. He is the best general counsel (GC) I could have asked to work under and to develop me, and is a source for most of the corporate practice lessons I hope to impart in this book.

The other person is my wife, who pestered me without end to write a book. I'm not sure why it was so darn important to her, but I could tell that if I didn't, she'd be disappointed. She has been the inspiration for so much of the success in my life that I'm not sure where I'd be without her. Thank you, Stephanie. You are my best friend, my life coach, and my forever love.

Lastly, I'd like to tell you that a great chapter in this book was removed in the review process. If you want to read it, shoot me an e-mail and I'll send it to you. Evidently, you can get a little too edgy, even for a tongue-in-cheek book such as this one.

William E. Kruse
Washington, DC

Introduction

"How'd you get that job?" Those were the words coming through the phone from one of my best friends. They were abruptly and almost immediately followed by something akin to, "Do they know you have no idea what you're doing?"

That was not how I intended to start my first day as a new corporate counsel. My days of brass-knuckled litigation were behind me,[1] and I was going to be living the good life in the hallowed halls of corporate America.

Now, one of my closest companions from law school, and someone who should have known my brilliance from all of those long evenings studying in the Keys and hearing me wax legal bloviations in class was not so subtly telling me I was about to start my first morning at my new job unprepared for what lay ahead. Was David Pollack[2] a better judge of my preparedness than my new employer?

My brain went into overdrive as I sat in a crowded downtown DC Dunkin' Donuts. I stared out the frosted window on that chilly February morning while sipping a warm coffee. Really, I just needed to kill time. I'll admit it. I was nervous, and I was way too early to start work. Maybe it was a remnant of my days on the Coast Guard cutter *Valiant*, where starting work at 0600 was the norm. I was reverting to habit and old routine in an effort to minimize extra things to think about.

---

1 Wrong, but that isn't the point of the book. Go back to the previous text.

2 Name not changed to protect the guilty. He should have known better than to scare the crap out of me on my first day. Who needs rude strangers when you have friends like this guy?

My "good luck" call with my friend hadn't made me any more comfortable. Just how early can you show up on your first day? I was pretty sure my new boss, the general counsel, wouldn't be at the office at 6:30 in the morning. Would the guard even let me in? What was I going to do when I got there? Would it be like my firm, with cases to work and client[3] work waiting for me? Or would I show up at my desk and not have anything to do? Would my future internal clients even know I was there to handle their pressing issues?

Well, that's a lot of rhetorical questions, but only half of the ones that were bouncing around in my head before the long walk down the block west of the Dunkin' Donuts. Boy, what I wouldn't have given to have a guidebook. I really just wanted to know what to expect. How would the interactions be different from the ones I was used to at my firm?

At the firm, it was simple. You worked with coworkers, and your clients were external. They came; they had needs. I worked on their issues, litigated them to resolution, and then worked on some other client's work. I didn't see that client every day in the hall. I didn't meet her husband and kids or get to know her personally the way you can only do when you see someone every day. This was going to be a completely different animal. I knew it, but I still didn't know how it was going to play out.

Come to find out, I wasn't alone. A few years into my time as a corporate counsel, I got a call. On the other end of the line was a very senior partner[4] at a well-respected firm in DC. She and I had worked on matters together over the years. We spent late nights on the phone going over the minutest details of pleadings, letters, and exhibits on serious, bet-the-company matters.

I trusted her judgment, respected her knowledge, and knew that she was an excellent lawyer. But here she was, telling me she had taken a position at a large defense contractor—their newest in-house counsel. She wanted help. The questions sounded very familiar. We were having coffee[5]

---

3 The intro is not too early for lesson number 1. As an inside counsel, you still have clients, but they are internal, and it will take you a long time to figure out who they are and the internal politics of why and what they really need.

4 This lawyer gets to remain anonymous.

5 Le Pain Quotidien. She was buying.

a couple days after our call, and I was being peppered with them. What the heck was she going to do? She only knew the politics of the firm. How would corporate life be different? What if she couldn't navigate the internal politics of her new internal clients? How was she going to handle a bad outcome on a matter for a client who more directly controlled her future than the external clients she was used to?

"I don't know why they didn't hand you a copy of the survival guide when they hired you," I joked over our coffee. But it was no joke. I still don't know why there isn't a survival guide for new in-house counsel. There are survival guides for far more mundane experiences. Do you really need a survival guide for navigating Paris? It's Paris for the love of all that's holy. You don't survive Paris; you eat everything, sightsee, and fall in love. There's also a survival guide for the zombie apocalypse. Zombies? A survival guide for zombies? Those don't even exist.

If Paris and zombies need survival guides, then taking a job as an in-house counsel sure the heck does. And so, here we are. I wrote one, and now you have one.

TIME TO GET YOUR BEARINGS: THE FIRST HUNDRED DAYS

It's Not My Circus and Those Are Not My Monkeys

Whatever you do, don't let other people make you their sheriff. Your new internal business partners are going to see you coming from a mile away. It doesn't matter how old or young you are. You can be an experienced former big law partner, or you can be right out of law school. You might have so much gray hair that it takes an entire case of Just for Men gel to look the ripe young age of eighty, or you might be so wet behind the ears that Niagara Falls couldn't keep up.

It won't matter. There will be a few dozen internal clients at your new corporate office who see you as their personal Johnnie Cochran and John Wayne all rolled into one. They have a hundred axes to grind and scores to settle. Other lawyers in the general counsel's office have blown them off or told them it wasn't a problem for the legal department. None of that will matter. You are new. You don't know any better. You will be anxious to help solve problems, and they smell your desperation for an issue to solve.

Don't fall prey. I had a friend who started at his company and had no idea what he was walking into. The general counsel saw himself as the next chief executive officer (CEO). The chief financial officer (CFO) and chief operating officer (COO) also saw themselves as the next CEO. There was a fight for resources across the board. Each silo of operations was in an internal struggle to climb the ladder of importance in the portfolio of company products and offerings. Spin-offs and acquisitions were ripe in the industry, and it was a struggle to remain the shiny offering in the 10K street report.

These weren't just internal struggles for dominance; they were career life-and-death to the combatants. For the winners, financial rewards, salary bumps, stock offerings, and job security. To the losers, jealousy and scheming if they were able to stay, and more likely the career search after being asked to resign. This is an extreme example, but there is some variation of this playing out in most companies today.

Some battles are minor skirmishes for resourcing between top sales executives. Some are as serious as those at my friend's new company. Either way, the battle is about to get a new front. At least one of the combatants, and maybe all of them, will see you as a shiny new tank division to be used in a flanking maneuver.

It starts so simply. You're being introduced to all your new colleagues in meeting after meeting. You're trying to impress and put your best foot forward. You want them to like you, as coworkers and future friends. You want them to respect you, as a lawyer and as a leader in the company. You want them to think more highly of you than your friend Dave[1] does, who we already established wasn't as impressed with your knowledge and potential ability as your new employer.

But they aren't just sizing you up. They are also trying to plant seeds in your head. They are valuable members of the team. They can help you navigate the treacherous uncharted waters you have just sailed into. This way, when they talk to you privately during the first lull in your first day, they can make you their sheriff. And there's always the same reason why.

They have reached a stalemate in the trench warfare of their interdepartmental struggle. They need someone to tell the other side that they should prevail. There is no more surefire way to succeed in that than to get an opinion from the legal department.

"I was just starting to see it your way, but Legal just let me know that what you wanted was illegal."

And with that, it will have become your circus, and they will now be your monkeys. It's too bad. It didn't have to be that way. You could have

---

1 If you don't know who Dave is, you should go back and read the intro. I worked hard on that section.

bought some time. So what should you do? First, listen, not just to the issue they are bringing you, but for clues that there is a backstory. You'll spot it if you listen carefully. It won't sound like what you are used to hearing at your firm from a new client. In those cases, you knew who the other side was. You might have had a client or two hide a ball every now and then, but you knew where to look and what questions to ask to get the whole story.

These situations are different. It won't be natural to assume that there is an ulterior motive and that there is an internal struggle at play. Your instinct might suggest to you that everyone inside the company has the same goals. Your instinct would be wrong. Listen for some key clues. They've been dealing with this for a while; it isn't that important, just trying to get your opinion. Or the really sneaky one, the casual question-drop on the way out the door after talking about nothing important at all, the sneaky back-door question.

When you get those, remember this advice: Don't bite. First, ask if they've already reached out to anyone else in Legal. We'll get to forum shopping later, but for now, just ask. Then ask them for some information they don't already have. At that point, one of two things will happen. Either they will go diligently search for the data or information you need and send it to you, or they will just go away. If it is the former, there is now a decent chance that it is an actual issue.[2] If it isn't, you will at least have more information to use in an effort to smoke out the potential internal conflict and decide if it is really a legal issue or just a business decision in search of legal cover.

If it is the latter, and they just go away, you have already navigated your first internal in-house minefield. You would be surprised how often people really just go away when asked to do just a little work before you have enough to help them. This is a telltale sign that it wasn't a real legal issue for you to deal with. If it is, they will be back.

This is harder than it sounds. You're new, and you want to help. You were hired for your knowledge and to solve problems. Turning people away seems counterintuitive. Don't let it be. You aren't turning them away.

---

2 This comes with a caveat. Don't be an idiot. A subpoena or allegations of internal problems that may be actual crimes require immediate attention. They won't go away. If they do, be even more afraid.

You are doing two things: (1) You are testing the issue to see if it really needs a legal opinion and you are actually doing your job; and (2) you are asking for the information you need to assist you in formulating an actual informed opinion. Rarely, if ever, will all the facts be present in your first meeting or by way of the first e-mail raising the issue.

This simple act will keep you from walking headfirst into an internal battle. You won't start your new career off as a sheriff in a business struggle that shouldn't be a legal issue, and you won't make enemies on your first day. It isn't your circus—don't accept the monkeys.

It's Amazing How Many Problems Go Away If You Just Do Nothing

Not everything is an emergency. The majority of the time, even the things that seem like emergencies have a way of working themselves out without intervention. There is a big difference between putting your head in the sand and keeping your eyes wide open and taking a pause before acting.

True emergencies require immediate attention. Is the building on fire? Are there armed agents from an overly acronymed agency at the reception desk? Worse yet, are those agents already searching another facility because the receptionist let them in and didn't think to call you first but now thinks it would have been a good idea? Those are emergencies. If one of those isn't happening, take a breath. Make those around you take a breath.

Rushing in may ease your deep desire to do something—to do anything. But it often just makes it worse. Sometimes, doing absolutely nothing is the best bet. Wait for the next move and then act, but act with thoughtful deliberation.

I'll give you an example. There was a time not long ago when the number of class actions over unsolicited faxes was rising faster than the temperature of Earth.[1] A few ~~jerks~~ well-intentioned home-based entrepreneurs thought that carpet-bombing potential customers with advertising

---

1 If you're a believer in that science about global warming. If not, it was rising faster than the temperature of the Saharan Desert at high noon.

faxes would grow their business. They never considered that the plaintiffs' bar members would support their new yacht addiction off the settlements that would follow.[2]

They also didn't seem to care that the law-abiding businesses that had sent legitimate faxes to actual customers would get caught in the cross fire. But alas, that was the situation. Pretty soon, every business that had ever sent a fax got a demand letter. It went something like this: "Pay a little now or else we will go after every fax you've ever sent at the statutory rate of $500 per fax, which we estimate will cost you $X million. Call immediately or we intend to file the attached complaint."

I know what you're thinking. It was the same thing that every business owner and inside counsel thought at the time:[3] "Oh crap! It's an emergency!" Well, it wasn't. It wasn't even close. It was a fishing expedition. Plaintiffs' lawyers were sending out demand letters to every company in every city that had ever sent a single fax. They couldn't work every case if they hired every unemployed lawyer laid off or whose hiring was deferred in the great law firm market correction of 2009–2010. It was impossible.

But you know what was possible? If you were a smart and entrepreneurial plaintiff lawyer, you would send thousands of letters and just wait for a couple of in-house counsel to call you. Now you had a fish on the line. You then let the ~~extortion~~ honest and fair legal process begin. The in-house counsel would explain that all their faxes were sent to existing clients in accordance with the law. And it would all go downhill from there. The costs start escalating, the demand gets larger, and pretty soon there is a class action with the company name all over it.

Do you know who wasn't sweating? The in-house counsel who did nothing. There were plenty of in-house attorneys who didn't rush in. They took a breath and did zero, zilch, nada. At least nothing visible. Like a duck on the water, all the action was occurring out of sight, under the water, out of view of our plaintiff's counsel. They looked into faxes sent to see if there was any actual exposure. They interviewed marketing managers and sales personnel to see if any had gone rogue and sent some unapproved

---

2 This isn't every plaintiff's lawyer, or even most. Our system needs someone to fight for the rights of those without power. But mass fax litigation? Come on.

3 Because I hadn't written this survival guide yet.

faxes. They calculated potential exposure and met with the exec team if it was in any way worrisome.

What didn't they do? They didn't pick up the phone. They took a breath and waited. Would a second notice come? Would a third? Chances were, there wouldn't be another notice. Why? Because the plaintiff's counsel was too busy gutting and skinning the poor fish that bit the hook. She didn't have enough lawyers on staff to work all the lines she dropped in the water. There was never an intention to work them all. They were chum in the water.

I'll give you another example. I was sitting on a nice seaside bench at an ABA TIPS meeting in San Diego on a break between meetings. A great business litigation attorney I know from Chicago was recounting his frustration about several young or new corporate counsels at clients' offices who would call him in a panic about receiving subpoenas from government agencies or from other law firms working on some business litigation matter. They were panicking and wanting action right away.

His frustration wasn't that he was going to bill hours and make money. That was fine, and he appreciated the tuition it would provide for the expensive private school for his daughter. He was more frustrated that these in-house counsel had forgotten so quickly how to handle a third-party subpoena once they went in-house. It didn't make sense. This was as simple as taking a breath and responding with a simple request to narrow the scope or objecting to an overly broad subpoena on a third party. It wasn't to rush in and start a massive document production operation.

They forgot, or never knew, that the best course of action was not to treat it as an emergency, but rather as a simple inconvenience. Breathe, take a moment, and see if it is even requiring a substantive response. Courts rarely make a nonparty go through an arduous production process if the request is unduly burdensome or the likely information is duplicative or can be gained by discovery from a party in the litigation.

Before treating it as an emergency and incurring internal costs and operational interruptions, think about picking up the phone and asking what the subpoenaing party really wants. You'd be surprised at how often it is just something small and inexpensive to gather. You'd also be surprised at how often they don't even know and couldn't articulate it at a hearing if you filed for a protective order. In which case, you're back to doing nothing.

Better yet would be looking to see if the subpoena was even valid. You'd be surprised how many aren't. Do you know what an improperly issued or served subpoena is in most jurisdictions? It's paper. It's nothing. It requires nothing. But knowing that requires taking a breath and looking into it before acting.

Either way, it's surprising how many problems go away if you just do nothing. Even if that nothing involved work behind the scenes that the creator of the problem never sees.

You'd Better Like What Your New Employer Does for Money

There is a funny thing about working at a firm. You get to do a little of everything. Sure, you might "just" be an antitrust lawyer, but you'll see anti-trust issues of every stripe. If you are a trial lawyer, you will feel integrated into a million different business types. Large, small, service, product, and everything in between. In my time as a law firm associate, I worked for and against just about every type of business and individual. I learned about coal bed methane rights in the Appalachians, union bargaining rights in railroad employment disputes, pharmaceutical research and development methods, rights in intellectual property, and just about every other thing you can imagine two entities fighting about.

The best part was that you couldn't get too bored. Even though I hated the pharmaceutical litigation, I learned a lot, and I had plenty of other really interesting things to research and work on that weren't in that industry. I spent a ton of time working on railroad and maritime issues, and I love trains and boats. That made the other cases on intellectual property less dreary.

But here's the thing about going in-house. Almost every business has a niche. They do one thing. That's the beauty of capitalism—specialization for maximum output. Very few of us will work at a multinational con-glomerate that does everything. Even if one of us did,[1] unless you are the

---

1 Okay. More than one of us will land this job. Maybe two of us?

general counsel or deputy general counsel, you aren't seeing everything across all the business lines; you are in a subsidiary that does one thing or things in one industry.

So what is the big deal? Well, you might assume that as an in-house counsel, it won't matter if you work for a bicycle company and don't have a passion for bikes. You're wrong. You will work on a ton of things for that company. That is true. Maybe you love intellectual property (IP) or love negotiating contracts. That is your new role at the company, so even though every single thing is about bikes, your day-to-day work is still something you enjoy.

There is just one problem with that. It will all be about bikes. I mean everything. The business disputes may be about shipping or packaging or IP, but it will be about bikes. Your coworkers will be passionate about cycling. They might wear spandex on their bike commute to the office and smell like sweat. No one else in the whole company will care, because they all love biking.

You will be pissed off in the elevator with a bunch of spandex-clad, sweating coworkers every morning. They will secretly judge you for driving everywhere and having a body fat percentage above single digits. Why? Passion.

You see, passion is different from being indifferent or even liking an industry or topic. If you are passionate about what your business does, you look at the contracts differently. You breathe the supply chain and care about distribution rights. You can't wait to see a new product launch and will stay late talking about work. Work won't even feel like work, because it is what you would be thinking about if you weren't at work.

You will be highly engaged if you love what your company does. The work matters not only because of the nature of your little role in the big picture, but also because the big picture is so important to you as a lawyer and as an employee.

I know what some of you are thinking. You want to go in-house, and you can't imagine passing up in-house jobs that are in boring industries just because the industry is boring to you. There are only two types of people I wrote this book for: those who just took an in-house job and those who think they want to go in-house. If you are looking for an in-house role, I implore you to narrow your search to things you love.

If you just took an in-house position, and you are reading this chapter thinking, *Oh, dang,* I'm sorry. There is hope, though, so long as you didn't take a job at a company or in an industry that you detest. If you just took a job at a clinical skin care company, for example, and are ambivalent about soap or skin toner, you don't have to quit your job just yet.

You can find passion. People fall in love with new hobbies all the time. Think about that time you fell in love with something. You couldn't read enough about it, watch enough movies about it, or talk to enough people about it. You are going to be working with people who are already passionate about what they do.[2] Talk to them. What do they love about it? What inspires them about the company's mission? Engagement and passion are infectious. Find the people who love what your company does and spend time with them. It will rub off, and ultimately, you will come to appreciate what you are doing, and your role will be much better for it.

---

2 Unless you work somewhere with a bunch of miserable and highly disengaged employees. Boy, I feel for you if that's the case. Get a shrink on speed dial. You'll need it and a bottle or two of bourbon.

Wait, What?
Do I Have B.O.?

Okay. This is going to sound ridiculous. Believe it or not, you will not have a lot of friends at first, maybe ever. At least, at work, that is.[1]

Let me take you on a little journey to my first work happy hour. Put on your imagination caps and come along as I weave a tale that leaves our poor protagonist sad, lonely, and dying of a broken heart. Not really that bad, but it was still a little awkward.

I hadn't been an in-house counsel very long when I caught wind of a company happy hour. It was a Thursday or Friday, and some colleagues were moving on to other jobs and some other new colleagues were just getting to know people at the office. Some young vibrant extrovert in admin services whipped up a nice invitation via e-mail, sent in HTML[2] with graphics and images, and very exciting.

I didn't know anyone yet, not really. I'm kind of outgoing, and I thought, *Bill, you old chap. You're going to go to this happy hour and make new work friends. While you're at it, bring your wife so she can meet people too.*

---

1 Or maybe you're not really the chummy chap type, and you couldn't care less. Don't worry, I won't judge.

2 I don't know how to do this. How does every person under the age of thirty know how to do this? Do they teach this in kindergarten now? I'm pretty sure my six-year-old nephew can do it.

And so I did. I called my wife and told her that we were going to Hill Country Barbecue in Penn Quarter. If you don't know DC, this is the very middle of the city. There are a ton of restaurants and bars, and I figured this place was about as casual as you could get, right? I mean, BBQ and beers—happy hour? How can you not make friends?

My wife showed up after work and met me at my office. We walked a block or two east and a block south. We were happy to be in a new city and happy to meet new friends. It had come fairly easy in the Coast Guard, and we were pretty used to meeting new people at new duty stations every few years. This wasn't a lot of pressure, and it was BBQ—and beers.

So we walk in, and I immediately notice that it is a little like a college party. First of all, the average age was slightly younger than I anticipated. It seems some of us get older as we move from our old lives, through a firm job, and settle into a corporate counsel role. Secondly, everyone is in little groups at different tables, and I really don't know anyone yet, so I am a little unsure—if I walk up to a table, they might not even work with me.

I finally see a couple young consultants from the floor at my office, which at least lets me know I'm in the right place. So Steph[3] and I do what we've done in countless situations just like this; we belly up to the table and start chatting with everyone. I introduce Steph, and then it happens. Every person at the table gets up and leaves.

I'm not kidding. They all had somewhere else to be other than with the new lawyer. One needed a beer; one needed to track down the waiter for the lost basket of brisket; one needed to go to the bathroom; one needed to take a call. You get the picture.

Never in my life had I cleared out an entire six-top in one sentence. I was a little floored. If I didn't already think so highly of myself, I would have been crushed. My wife, my amazing wife, laughed at me right then and there. I can still hear her in my ear saying, "HAHAHA. No one likes you."[4]

I got myself a beer and some pulled-pork sliders, and Steph and I enjoyed a six-top table to ourselves. After beer number two, I was able to laugh at the very idea that a bunch of young professionals would be

---

3 Steph is my amazing, awesome, gorgeous wife.

4 It may have been a little less cold than that, but it's the message I got.

cool having one of the new in-house counsel crash their happy hour. I was being a total idiot to think they would want me around.

The next day, it really sank in. There weren't going to be a whole lot of people from work who were ever going to feel comfortable hanging out with me. No matter how much I grew on them, they would always see me as part of the senior staff. I might get invited to a big gathering that a lot of the office would attend, but I wouldn't be getting e-mails around 4:45 p.m. saying it was time to sneak out early and get a beer.

To this day, the invitations I get to dinner or to have a Saturday beer is with the general counsel.

This little bit of distance isn't actually all that bad. You want to be social and get along with your internal clients and colleagues. You want to build rapport and trust, and you want to build relationships. But you also want them to understand that you might have to represent the company, and it might not always be in the direction they prefer.

Some organizations are extremely hierarchical. Some are as flat as the state of Florida. In some hierarchical companies, this will be forced on you and it might feel like the military. You won't even be allowed to hang out or socialize with junior staff. I am not a real fan of that model, but it works for some companies; it's their culture.

Even in a pancake-flat organization, you're going to run into this a little. It will take years to establish real friendships. I'm just writing this to let you know it isn't you. You don't stink. People just want to figure out their boundaries with the legal team on their own terms. Once you notch them a few wins, and they feel you are in their corner, the long-time employees will start to want you around more and more. Just don't expect a whole lot of dinner-and-a-movie invites.

What Do You Mean It Is Being Made by Slaves?!?

Can you imagine the morning that the GC of one of the major food suppliers received news that almost every shrimp consumed by every American was caught by and processed by slaves? I can just picture him, sitting on his sofa, with his fluffy dog, sipping coffee and wearing ugly plaid sleepy pants.

He probably envisioned a relaxing morning of sipping dark black coffee,[1] taking in his stack of morning news while CNN played in the background. He might have had some e-mails to catch up on, a litigation brief to review, and maybe even some due-diligence reports to review on an upcoming merger or acquisition.

And then, like getting slapped in the face with a wet fish, his relaxing morning was interrupted by a news headline that slavery was alive and kicking. Not just that, but that it was his industry—international food—that was allegedly one of the big violators of international human rights.

This had to absolutely ruin his morning. The headline from the *Guardian* that broke the six-month investigation really said it all:

Revealed: Asian slave labour producing prawns for supermarkets in US, UK
Thai 'ghost ships' that enslave and even kill workers are linked to global shrimp supply chain, Guardian investigation discovers

---

1 Once again, this is the only way to drink coffee. I'm sorry, but if you need cream and sugar, you just don't actually like coffee.

- Trafficked into slavery on Thai trawlers to catch food for prawns
- Thailand's seafood industry: state-sanctioned slavery?
- Ask your questions—live chat as it happened"[2]

It was immediately followed by multiple nationwide articles:

From the *Washington Post*: Don't Eat That Shrimp!
From the *Atlantic*: Walmart, Whole Foods, and Slave Labor Shrimp
From the AP: Seafood from Slaves

In short, it was a bad time to be in the food sourcing business, especially if that sourcing involved seafood—double so if it involved shrimp.

Do you know what follows news stories like these? Investigations from states' attorneys general, investigations from Congress, lawsuits by class-action plaintiff's counsel, and letters from clients demanding to know why your company is selling them slave-caught seafood.

If one of these corporate counsel is really unlucky, they're also selling food on military bases or some other government establishment and have now opened themselves up to being included on a list of suspended or debarred contractors for having unethical business practices.

It isn't just food, and not just companies with international supply chains that are at risk. There was a very well-known hotel chain that found itself in a bit of a lurch a couple years back as well. Turns out, some maids aren't here in Middle America cleaning rooms entirely of their own volition. Actually, they are often hired as employees of separate 1099 contractors, and some of those "contractors" are really just slave pimps.

They quite literally were using force, or threat of force, on the families of the maids to hold them against their will and turn them loose on our hotel rooms at little to no pay. At some of these hotels, they would work long shifts and then be collected in a van to a hotel on a less ritzy side of town where they would be crammed into one room to share.

Until they work off their "debt," which like my credit card balance in college never seems to go down, they aren't free to leave, to quit, to work

---

2 This headline was from the *Guardian*'s online version of its story on June 10, 2014: www.theguardian.com/global-development/2014/jun/10/ supermarket-prawns-thailand-produced-slave-labour.

somewhere else, or even find their own living accommodations or meals. So the "debt" grows, and they work cleaning our rooms.

One day, someone figures it out. Do you know who isn't in trouble? The contractor with the slave labor. He's out of business and out of town at the first hint of trouble. You know who is in trouble? The hotel chain. Even if they aren't in legal trouble, which in today's more vigilant climate they will be, they are in public relations (PR) trouble.

Do you know where no one wants to sleep? In a bed cleaned and turned down by slaves, that's where. So when the news breaks that some hotel is using a contractor to clean rooms staffed by slaves, the GC better act fast.

Which is a long road to my point. The time to act has already passed. Think of your new in-house role like the start of a new administration. What do you want to do in your first hundred days? Those first hundred days of a new presidential administration set the tone for any president's next four years.

In the same manner, what you decide to do in your first hundred days will set the tone for your time as an in-house counsel at your new company. I could provide you a million suggestions, and probably will eventually. Here is one to start out on pretty quickly: Look at your supply chain, now!

You might be going to a very sophisticated organization with a supplier due-diligence process that is spickety-span clean. Well good for you. Most new in-house counsel aren't so lucky. I have news for you. Even if the policy they show you on day one seems perfect, half of you are walking into organizations where what is going on isn't what the policy says anyway.

So make it a priority. While you are learning everything about your new company, its operations, billing procedures, future plans, and culture, also learn about the supply chain. Don't just take anyone's word for anything. When they say they know where the screws that hold the chairs together come from, ask them how they know. It seems small and miniscule, but it will pay dividends in the future.

If you do this right, your management committee will never wake up to a news report that one hundred Bangladeshi workers burned alive because they were locked in a room to sew your company's hoodies all day and not allowed to leave. This sounds dark, but it isn't all unicorns and rainbows in international business. You have an obligation to recognize this risk and address it.[3]

---

3 In my mind, you have a responsibility to do this as a human being too.

MANAGING THE INTERNAL CRISIS

You Are Always the Center of Your Own Crisis; No One Else Notices or Cares 90 Percent of the Time

You know how it happens. A company either gets sued by a client or vendor or is named by a government agency in a probe of the government cause du jour.[1] Not only is it a concern for the legal team, but also for the executive committee and potentially the board. And trust me, to each one of those constituents, they feel like the company and the brand are in the spotlight.

I'll share a little secret that a great public relations damage control expert told me once. No one notices or even cares. Just because it is the only thing going on in your life doesn't mean everyone else is paying attention. Everyone else is too busy to notice.

Now, that's not always the case, but it's absolutely the case about 90 percent of the time. Unless you are Volkswagen (VW) in 2016, and every paper in the world has been running a dozen stories a day about how dishonest you are, and how your top engineers are big fat liars and a little dishonest. We may find out that the engineers at VW didn't really program defeat devices into clean diesel models in an attempt to make the nitrous oxide gas emissions seem low enough to pass inspection. But the damage was done in the media already.

---

1 These are usually less appetizing than the soup du jour, and usually much more expensive. Don't order these.

The only other case that comes to mind in vivid exception to the rule is the Deepwater Horizon riser pipe failure. You can't live stream oil pouring into the gulf for eighty-seven days straight on CNN and not expect to take a hit to your reputation. But those are the exceptions that prove the rule. We only remember them because they were so egregious and so promoted on a daily basis for news cycle eternity. You won't remember that ACME and Generico, Inc., also had reputation problems at the same time.

But all that offers little solace to the personnel at companies dealing with a crisis. When they were going through it, the glare of the spotlight loomed large. It felt as if every small news story, even in a local paper, were being read by every customer, potential investor, and especially every competitor. In fact, it wasn't. Oh, there were a couple of those people who came across it, but it wasn't the white-hot glare of the sun that those inside believed it would be.

So what's the point? It's not like knowing this makes it any better. Well, for one, it keeps you from violating the survival point in a chapter before. You won't go rushing into a solution to a problem that might be better solved by ignoring a reporter and doing nothing. Getting ahead of a story sometimes makes it a story.

There are whole books on this topic, and if you're in the situation where a company issue will make negative press, I'd encourage you to read one immediately. I won't get into every theory and detail; that's why there are public relations damage-control experts. I will give you some advice to get you through all but the worst situations, though:

1. Reporters are not your friends. Unless they are actually your friends. Were you in his wedding? Did he buy your kid a birthday present last year? No, then you aren't friends. Don't make the mistake of thinking the reporter is friendly. He won't write this story the same way he wrote the last business article you read of his. You have no idea what he's going to write.

2. Since you and the reporter aren't friends, don't talk to him like he's a friend. Don't speak off the cuff or unprepared. Best not to speak at all. He has e-mail. It's much harder over e-mail than over the phone to get a little extra line out of you that you'll regret later.

3. Prepare early. Once you know there is an issue that has any chance of getting a single drop of ink, get a core team together to prepare

for the storm, even if the odds are great the storm will eventually blow out to sea without touching you. Besides legal, you need someone from the executive leadership team, especially someone who handles press inquiries. If you don't know who that person is, find out who answers the Contact Us line from the company website. They'll either know or it's them. Don't laugh; you'd be surprised.

4. Once you have a team put in place, start running what-if scenarios. What if a reporter gets ahold of the complaint from the courthouse? What if a reporter calls someone at the Department of Justice (DOJ) or the Security and Exchange Commission (SEC)? What happens if the plaintiff's counsel calls a plaintiff-friendly reporter and gives up a copy of the complaint with an interview of the plaintiff? It's time to have one or two lines written up for every scenario you can imagine.

   When and if the facts change, or new parties or issues arise, repeat Step 4 again. Heck, you should repeat Step 4 at least every Friday before you leave the office just to make sure the prepared statements are still what you want to say. Also, they won't release a story on Friday if it's real news. They'll wait until the next week when they have a chance to make a bigger splash.

5. After you have the scenarios in place and answers to any possible line of inquiry, you wait, and you only release what you've prepared if it's asked for. If at all possible, control your executives. You have to keep them from making a statement outside of what's prepared. They'll think they are helping. They aren't. Before you know it, that nice chat they had that will set the reporter straight about the facts turns into another story that should already be dead, breathing new life into it with additional runway to spare. It'll be hard, but you have to keep them in line. This will be the most painful part.

6. How do you keep executives in line? You remind them of the central premise. You are always the center of your own crisis—no one else notices or cares 90 percent of the time. This is going to be hard. No one believes that. They want the world to hear their side of the story. That's the wrong path almost every time. If you think this time is the exception, you're probably wrong.

It Is a Capital Mistake to Theorize Before You Have All the Evidence

So said Sir Arthur Conan Doyle in "A Scandal in Bohemia."

I, for one, have never made this mistake.[1] If we were all rational human beings, we wouldn't need a chapter on this. Alas, we aren't rational. We are anything but. So, here we are. I'm writing this and you are reading it thinking that it is too obvious to warrant a brief chapter in this brief book. You're wrong.

You see, we all do this. We do it every day. It is how we get through life. When we are young, it takes us forever to get anything done. We have to learn, literally everything. After a while, we start to reason and make inferences and judgments based on intuition and repeatable patterns. It's how we get through the day without getting run over by a bus.[2]

When I walk my dog and we come across a straggly, crooked stick of just the right length at dawn or dusk, we both jump just a little. We are wired to think it is a snake. Judging before we have the facts keeps her paws and mine from getting bit by the ferocious stick beast. We feel stupid after we realize it is just a stick. I even look around to see if anyone saw me looking like a fool. The dog? She doesn't seem to care.

---

1 I'm clearly lying. We have all done this, or we wouldn't need a chapter on it.

2 Okay. Most of us. The Darwin Awards only exist to reward those who don't fit this pattern and who do, in fact, get run over by buses that most of us would have avoided.

But this intuition, leaping-to-conclusions type of behavior doesn't really work very well in the law department atmosphere. We don't just look stupid when we make this mistake, but we also put the company and our friends and colleagues at risk. I'm not advocating paralysis by analysis, but we need to get pretty far down the fact train track before we start drawing conclusions.

So, here's a story. I don't pretend to write as well as Sir Doyle, but you're stuck with me, so I hope you like it. If not, tough luck, there aren't any refunds on the book.

On top of being a lawyer, I have a friend who was also his organization's compliance officer. That is a role similar to mine. Both he and I see lots of interesting things. We see things that walk like a duck, talk like a duck, and then end up being a fish. That's to say, nothing is ever as it seems at first.

One day, he's working on regular, fun, in-house legal work.[3] His contracts manager, who is extremely social and has a slight flair for the dramatic, burst into his office like her hair is in a state of fire that is so hot and bright, it has become invisible to everyone but her. Her voice has a little crack that indicates the sky is also falling. According to her, an account might have been billed for deliverables not done. The company might not have intended to do them at all.

Well, the rational person would start looking for more facts and not assume that a company would just decide to bill and not do work. But we already established that humans aren't all that rational, and sometimes get a lot spooked at a little stick that might have fangs. Well, when you bill the US government for work that hasn't been done, they use a stick called the False Claims Act, and it has fangs.

So, my friend starts shooting off e-mails and demanding answers. He wants to find out what happened, but he also already has his mind made up that something is actually amiss. The account in question was always causing him some grief. The contract was in a constant state of flux and it wasn't hard to imagine a billing error occurring.

---

3 You will have fun in-house work. If not, leave. Life's too short to only do boring, bland paper pushing. Unless the economy tanks again and you need to feed your family. Then I'm sorry. You're just stuck.

Before long, the project manager's boss is involved, the head of government sales is involved, the head of operations at a different city center is involved, and everyone is spending time that can't be billed to a client to investigate an allegation that work had been billed for that no one intended to perform.

There was only one problem. It wasn't factually accurate. The running theory being investigated was that the team needed to make a deadline and just decided they would perform an extra deliverable in the next option year of the contract. Push out one report that the client didn't really know they were owed. The bill could be sent on time, and no one would be the wiser.

The theory was wrong. There was no deliverable due. The project manager was on schedule and the invoice was accurate. My friend managed to get a whole lot of people very worried because he got caught up in the hysteria that something must have happened. He lost track of the principle not to freak out without all the facts.

There are worse stories. I've committed worse infractions of this rule.[4] We all have. Take the time to calmly look at things before jumping to conclusions. Every once in a while, a stick really is a snake. Most of the time, though, it's just a stick.

---

4 No way I'm copping to them in a book. Are you nuts?

Conflagration

Fires happen. Mass conflagration is often the result of unforced errors. For those who don't know what a mass conflagration is, I'll explain.

The first ship I reported to upon enlisting in the Coast Guard was the Coast Guard cutter *Valiant*. She was home ported in Miami, Florida, and was for all intents and purposes ancient. Her keel was laid about a decade before I was conceived. She wasn't modern, or sleek, or comfortable.

The funny thing about older vessels is that they need a lot of upkeep. We spent a ton of time just keeping her fit to sail. She was the crew's home. I spent the equivalent of seven months a year sleeping on board. We were deployed most of the time, and when in port, she still needed a crew to watch over her and maintain her.

As a part of the process of reporting to any ship in the fleet, you spend the first three months learning basic damage control and the next three months learning advanced damage control techniques. There is a reason for this. It is your floating home. There is no fire department to call if an emergency occurs. Unlike your home on land, you can't just climb out a window, call 911, and wait across the street while it goes up in flames.

If you attempt that at sea, you end up adrift in the ocean. Do you know how big the ocean is? Nine-foot waves that looked okay from the upper deck of a ship look really terrifying when crashing down on a life raft with no land for hundreds of miles. It's much better to learn how to defend the ship and keep it afloat, since no one else is coming to rescue you.

So, you report on board and they hand you a blank sheet of paper and a pen and tell you to trace the fire control system of the entire cutter. If you are an engineer, this might not seem so daunting. For everyone else, a strange look of confusion is the first indication that tracing fire control systems is not something we have been trained on.

I spent weeks trying to trace the pipes that deliver lifesaving water to fire hoses in the event that any space on the ship decided to spontaneously combust. I crawled in tight spaces in the belly of the ship. I looked in the overheads[1] and scoured every square inch of every deck on that ship trying to figure out exactly where all of the water pipes went that made up this fire-suppression system. It was almost impossible.

After that, each of us needed to build on our firefighting knowledge taught in boot camp. We had to figure out how to fight fuel fires, break into compartments and rescue shipmates, deflood a space to keep the ship afloat, and how to keep each other alive. The biggest thing we were working on, whether we realized it or not, was preventing a mass conflagration.

I don't know about you, but I had never heard of mass conflagration before spending my time on the *Valiant*. Conflagration is fire, but not just any fire. It is a series of fires, spreading rapidly and out of control from space to space, compartment to compartment and deck to deck. It causes noxious fumes and lots of smoke, and it leads to water damage and potentially explosions, human casualties, and a host of problems that might put the ship and the entire crew's lives at risk. It is essentially a bad situation from which horrible outcomes are almost inevitable.

The first time I heard the term was during a training exercise out at sea. We ran a mass conflagration drill, and it was horrible. Everything that could go wrong did. We lost power; we lost propulsion. The engine room became a death chamber for the engineers. We were sinking and ended up in an abandon ship drill with well under a full complement of crew. Had this been real life, those would have been my friends dying. I felt lucky it was just a drill.

Right about now you might be wondering why we are spending so much time talking about life on a ship fighting make-believe fires. Isn't this

---

1 That's a ceiling. Bulkheads are walls, and decks are floors.

supposed to be a book about surviving your role as an in-house counsel? Yes. It is, and this story is quite illustrative of a few keys to your success:

1. **Prepare ahead. Look for weak spots.**
2. **Think about how one fire can spread.** What are the potential consequential damages that can rage out of control if not handled quickly?
3. **Trace out your damage-control resources in advance.** Know where every possible spot in the organization is that might have the resource you need to put out the fire. The time to do this is well in advance of the emergency. Don't find yourself looking for a lifesaving resource after the fire has started.
4. **It takes a team to keep a fire contained.** While you might be ready, have you trained those just reporting on board? Do they know how to immediately pitch in and prevent the spread of a disaster? You need to train them how to make things better and not worse when the smoke and fire rear up from behind a bulkhead.
5. **The most important thing you can do when an emergency situation arises is keep it under control.** Do not let it spread or it will be like a contagion. It will infect the organization and snowball until you end up abandoning ship with massive casualties.

There is one more lesson that transfers well from the CGC *Valiant* to your role as corporate counsel. One of the most important things to do during a crisis is execute a plan you have already put into place. Plan for breaches in your IT security defenses, plan for a client to sue you in public, plan on a government investigation. Map it out. What would you do? Have a communication plan in place with senior management with some baseline ideas of how to proceed.

Do all of this with an eye on preventing a small situation, a minor trash can fire, from burning your whole organization to the ground. When the ship sinks, there will be sharks in the water. It never gets better once you've lost control. Prevent the conflagration.

Don't Overreact

There was a time, long before I was in the practice of law, when a letter from a law firm to a small business or a one-man operation would immediately stoke fear and compliance with any demand.

"It has come to my attention that you are stealing from my client. If you don't knock it off, we are going to sue you immediately and make sure you never work again." Or something like that. You get the point. The "little guy" would be beat into submission, would stop selling his knock-offs, and would just go away.

Then came the Internet—Twitter and Facebook in particular. Never before could so much outrage spread so fast based on so few facts. Some of my favorite morning reading is the latest moral outrage over some corporate giant doing the horrible injustice of asking an IP thief to stop stealing.

One of the backfires that comes to mind is the "Eat More Kale" debacle for Chick-fil-A. I don't know how much you know about Vermont, but apparently they like local produce and local art and like to have a little fun at the expense of big food companies.

There was a guy in Vermont who had a local T-shirt and bumper sticker business called Eat More Kale. This promoted local Vermont farmers, and for most people seemed at most a little bit of parody on Chick-fil-A's eat more chicken campaign.

So Chick-fil-A did what any big nationwide company would do, right? They sent a "Get off my lawn" letter. It included the standard language and demanded he send all of his merchandise to Georgia to be destroyed.

That did not work out so well for Chick-fil-A. It seems that people had a lot more compassion for the Kale man than the big company who they thought was stomping on the little guy. Pretty soon, the following letter went up on Change.org:

I just signed the following petition addressed to: To: CHICK-FIL-A's Management Team.

Please quit blocking EATMOREKALE.COM's federal trademark application.

This petition is against corporate bullying. Vermont's own EAT MORE KALE is a small, quirky family business. The business's owner, Bo Muller-Moore, makes one-at-a-time, hand-printed t-shirts that express support for local agriculture and community farmers' markets. EAT MORE KALE is attempting to secure a federal trademark for the business name they've been using for more than ten years.

But Corporate Goliath fast food chain CHICK-FIL-A has threatened to block their attempt and shut them down, alleging that EAT MORE KALE confuses CHICK-FIL-A customers and dilutes their multi-million dollar industry.

Bo Muller-Moore makes eco-friendly t-shirts that support sustainable agriculture—his business is no threat to a multi-million dollar fast food company.

Please stop your corporate bullying of small businesses. Please immediately halt your actions to block EAT MORE KALE's federal trademark.

This letter has been signed over 42,000 times. Not only did it blow up in Chick-fil-A's face, but also the letter itself led to the opposite thing that Chick-fil-A wanted. Instead of stopping this small business, they brought national attention to him. He sold a ton of shirts and bumper stickers.

Eventually, Chick-fil-A ended up being the one having to go on the defense, justifying all of the negative publicity in an increasingly losing battle. They were being socially shamed for defending their brand.

It isn't that they shouldn't defend their turf. They just went about it all wrong. They could have handled it like the big company they were and not punched down. Recently, Jack Daniel's figured out that if you send nice cease-and-desist letters, you might just win more fans instead of being Twitter-shamed.

Some guy wrote a book. He designed the book cover and it looked just a little too much like a Jack Daniel's bottle label. I suspect that someone in the legal team immediately whipped up a really crotchety "screw you for stealing from us" letter. But instead, maybe they had a couple rounds of Jack and Coke and calmed down.[1] After sleeping on it, they sent a cease-and-desist letter begging to be shared on Twitter:

> It has recently come to our attention that the cover for your book *Broken Piano for President*, bears a design that closely mimics the style and distinctive elements of the Jack Daniel's trademarks.
>
> We are certainly flattered by your affection for the brand, but while we can appreciate the pop culture appeal of Jack Daniel's, we also have to be diligent to ensure that the Jack Daniel's trademarks are used correctly. Given the brand's popularity, it will probably come as no surprise that we come across designs like this one on a regular basis. What may not be so apparent, however, is that if we allow uses like this one, we run the very real risk that our trademark will be weakened. As a fan of the brand, I'm sure that is not something you intended or would want to see happen.
>
> In order to resolve this matter, because you are both a Louisville "neighbor" and a fan of the brand, we simply request that you change the cover design when the book is reprinted. If you would be willing to change the design sooner than that (including on the digital version), we would be willing to contribute a reasonable amount towards the cost of doing so. By taking this step, you will help us to ensure that the Jack Daniel's brand will mean as much to future generations as it does today.
>
> We wish you continued success with your writing and we look forward to hearing from you at your earliest convenience.

It was signed by Christy Susman, one of Jack Daniel's legal counsel for trademark protection.[2]

Not only did the company come off as calm, cool, and collected, but the letter also offered to help pay to have this author change his book cover. Jack Daniel's didn't demand he destroy his inventory, and they didn't say it in overly lawyerly threatening language. They treated him with respect

---

1 I have no actual facts that support this version of events. In my imagination, it is how it went down. Just roll with it.

2 http://www.abajournal.com/news/article/jack_daniels_cease-and-desist_letter _goes_viral_for_being_exceeedingly_poli.

and instead of catching all hell over it from the Internet mob, they were rewarded with positive feedback as the note spread on multiple websites and blogs.

The moral of the story is that you can protect your brand and also be a decent human being. You can serve your client's interest a lot better by not overreacting. Next time you are ready to fire off an overly lawyerly letter to a small business, remember Jack Daniel's. Pour a Jack and Coke, and calm down before you fire it off. You might just serve your client and get some free good publicity in the process.

They Are Watching You for Signs of Whether Everything Is Okay or Whether the Ship Is Sinking with No Life Rafts

To put it bluntly, you are their canary in the coal mine. If you are tense, they sense it. If you are at ease and don't think anything of the current situation, they will calm down almost immediately. If they don't, you need to let them in on this secret, because others in the organization will be looking at them for this same weather forecast. The COO's operations folks will be looking at her to know whether it is smooth sailing or time to batten down the hatches.

When revenue is flat and earnings per share are going in the wrong direction,[1] people look to the business side of the house for answers and comfort. Is the CFO worried? Is the COO looking at a reduction in force?[2] Or are they totally chill? They must know that everything's okay. They wouldn't be so calm if this was a trend. It must just be a blip. I'm sure revenue and earnings will improve soon.

See how that works? Except when the issue is legal in nature, they won't be looking at the CFO. They'll be secretly watching you. They'll watch you get coffee. They'll watch you interact and laugh with coworkers at the café vending machine. They'll see if you are more stressed or locked

---

1 Down. Down is the wrong direction for earnings. I know you went to law school and are not an accountant, but this one should be common sense. You shouldn't need a footnote for this one.

2 You'll hear the term RIF. Act like you've heard it before. It's a layoff.

up in your office more than usual. Believe me, they are watching everything. They are looking for guidance in your behavior.

So how do you project reassurance and calm? Well, for starters, you don't act much differently than you do on any other day. If you answer "Great" to every casual greeting on a normal workday, don't switch to, "Okay" or, "I'm making it" when the company is facing legal headwinds. These little, subtle messages mean a lot more to the team than you realize.

It's okay to have emotions. We aren't zombies.[3] Real, living beings have emotions we can't control. We have bad days. But we can be cognizant and aware of signals we are sending that can be misinterpreted by people looking to us as leaders in the organization.

I didn't realize this soon enough, so I'm trying to save you the headache. Once, I had just settled a business litigation matter for an amazing outcome. I was happy, and showing my emotions on my sleeve. I was taking off early to celebrate, hat, gloves, and scarf in hand. I couldn't have been outwardly showing how happy I was any more if I was whistling and a three-piece brass band was following me as an entourage.

Then it happened. My CEO's executive assistant showed up with a folder full of bad news that I knew was going to screw up not just my celebratory night, but also my foreseeable future. I was pissed. I let everyone know it. The aforementioned band came to a screeching halt, and I threw my scarf and hat back into my office as a string of curse words flew out of my mouth.

The impact on those around me was instantaneous. While the issue that arrived with a thud in my life wasn't the end of the world to me or the company, people assumed it was. I had let my emotions get the best of me. The obvious fall from such a high to such a low was too much for people to see and not notice. Word spread like wildfire and people were scared. It took a long time to convince everyone that everything was all right.

We lost a lot of productivity in the days that followed until people could be reassured that the world wasn't crumbling and that we weren't going to have a company-ending legal matter on our hands. Don't make that mistake. Keep calm and act normal, even when you are feeling the pressure or are really worried. You're a leader, not just a lawyer. Act like it.

---

3 Yes, zombies will come up again.

HOW DO YOU GET ANYTHING DONE?

Why Do We Care?

We've all been there. You get to the end of a long meeting. You've hashed out the way forward. Everyone knows, or thinks they know, the plan and their role. But is it all worth it? What are the end results we really want to achieve? Do they fit the organization's strategic purpose?

Sometimes we can get caught up in the process, in the minutia of getting through the day, week, or month. We can lose track of where the piece we are working on fits into the bigger picture. Before long, we are scheduling meetings and laying out solutions to situations that might not even be relevant to the direction and goals of the organization overall.

I'll give you an example. Let's just assume you work for a tech industry giant on the cutting edge of research with the best consumer products. Your legal team is always trying to stay steps ahead of the challenges and is proactive at protecting your organization's trade secrets, methods, processes, and overall business. One tool in your kit that comes in handy is proactive litigation to prevent competitor theft and use of your intellectual property.

Pretty soon, the process of handling the cases takes on a life of its own. You have regular status meetings on new potential infringements as well as meetings on the direction and potential outcomes of pending injunction actions.

Then imagine that one day, a bright junior associate counsel speaks up at the very end of the meeting. She's a little afraid to ask this, but can't help herself: "Why do we care?" And do you know what? It'll be the best question asked in one of these meetings in years.

Too often, we lose track of the big picture. But this one simple question can refocus the part that the issues discussed in that meeting have on the overall corporate strategy. Or better yet, they may expose that the entire exercise was a waste of everyone's time.

Let's just assume that our brave junior counsel hasn't been there long enough to go on autopilot and keep working without asking her all-important question. So during the meeting, she can't help but wonder why the organization keeps fighting so hard on an aging business process that was on the way out the door. The company is already on a path to a different tech solution and pretty soon the items being stolen and resold won't be worth it anyway.

She might be wondering why the company isn't looking at better IP protection strategies that made more sense for a mature product that was on its way to obsolescence. She is probably asking herself why she isn't getting real, meaningful work done instead of sitting through a waste of a status meeting, knowing happy hour would start an hour earlier if she could get this hour of her life back.

But too often, people won't ask, "Why do we care?" It's too important not to ask. Are we just spinning our wheels? Has this strategy outlived its usefulness? Is what we are doing still aligned with the organization's goals overall? The answers might all lead to the conclusion that the meeting was useful and the goals and directions are worthy of pursuit. Or it may redirect resources by refocusing what is really important. So be like our young associate counsel. At the end of a meeting you know is a waste of time, ask, "Why do we care?"

If you aren't ever in meetings where you aren't dying to ask this question, you aren't getting yourself into enough of your organization's meetings. But that's a whole other chapter.

Don't Focus on the Words They Use. What Do They Really Want?

If your in-house job ends up anything like mine, you will most certainly have a whole lot of contracts to review. You will see contracts for vendors, contracts from clients, contracts with the contingent workforce, contracts with real estate developers, and contracts to make contracts. I wish you the best of luck that you don't detest contracts with all of your heart by the time you retire.

Here is the funny thing they don't tell you about contracts in law school. You have a contract because you have two parties who ultimately want to get something done. We end up spending so much time making sure that the elements of a contract are present,[1] and so much time on all of the arbitration clauses and the deadlines and the liquidated damages clauses, that we often forget that our client and the other party just want to get a job done.

You are going to run across a project one day, and it will end up taking as long to negotiate the contract as the project is supposed to take to complete. That is not efficient and it certainly doesn't make the salespeople happy. Why in the world do we even go through that exercise? I know what you're thinking: "If I don't, how am I actually protecting the company?" But you really need to ask yourself this: "If you are spending this

---

1 Okay. At least in law school.

much time negotiating words in a contract that may never come into play, are you really serving the interests of your clients?" After all, one party wants some work done, and the other one just wants to do the work and make some money.

I will never forget one time having to spend quite a few nights negotiating a contract at 1:00 a.m. that was going to take place half a world away. I would set my alarm for 11:00 p.m. to start reviewing my notes and start drinking a ton of coffee and then getting on the phone with lawyers nine time zones away in order to argue about the definitions of data and the difference in arbitration from one locale to another. Meanwhile, my company and the other organization just wanted to get started.

I will always remember my Eureka moment. We were four nights into this nightly exercise, and I was low on sleep, tired, and fed up. I finally asked the other lawyer, "I see the words that you keep trying to use, but what do you actually mean? What is your real concern?"

After that, the floodgates of productivity opened and we were on our way. Both of us were way too busy being entrenched in our own feelings about things we would never agree to. Once we started talking about what each of us really needed and what we were trying to accomplish, we could find a way to state it and find middle ground.

Ultimately, if you can get to a place where you understand what somebody wants the words to mean, what they want this clause to achieve, you can just write that down in plain English. Pretty soon, you realize that you have spent a whole lot of time arguing over semantics. You also just might realize that the things you've been fighting against don't have a real basis for worry based on the risk profile of the project.

This also comes in handy when working with your salespeople. They will often have a hard time trying to set up the structure of a deal. They will put into place all kinds of crazy mechanisms to trigger payment or fees for a cancellation or strange methods of transferring rights in data or deliverables. Pretty soon, you don't even know what you are trying to negotiate. They have confused you[2] with the words they keep using and you better sit down and ask them what they want the contract to really mean.

---

2 Don't worry. They are confused; the client is now confused. Everyone is confused.

They usually go on and on about how there will be a right to the product but only if the client stays a client for so long and then only if they exceed a certain delivery threshold followed by getting you at least X number of new clients and then they will share in the revenue that will reduce their billables—and the confusion will only get deeper from there. That is the precise moment for the question,

"What do you actually want to achieve?"

"Let me help you write that in plain English."

You will find that what they really are trying to do is ensure the client stays on for a long enough period of time to recoup investment or has some skin in the game. Or come to find out they are trying to structure a joint venture and it's not really a client at all. These are the things you need to figure out up front. Otherwise, you are going to spin your wheels at 1:00 a.m. a whole lot of nights.

In this job, it can get way too easy to think we are just reviewing a contract. We aren't. We are structuring deals and protecting the company. We are also laying the foundation for a project. These contracts are the blueprints for future work. Imagine a blueprint where the architect didn't understand the support necessary for a wing of a house. It would be a disaster. We need to get it right up front. In order to do that, we need to not be confused by the words but rather know what they need them to mean.

Be Open to the Possibility That You Are Completely Wrong

I know that you believe you are always right. We all do. I myself have actually never been wrong about anything.[1] However, other people, I've been told, need to understand that they aren't always right.

My boss recently told me that he was reading a great book, and one of the chapters was all about how the absence of evidence doesn't mean that the evidence is absent.[2] After you get done clearing your head from the weird double-negative quasi-consciousness of that, it starts to make sense.

It reminds me of a story I heard about a leadership team and a legal department going head over heels to save an employee. Hold on to your hat. This one's a doozy.

You see, companies go to great lengths to save key employees. They are diamonds. They are special snowflakes. Pick your metaphor. The point is, they are always "irreplaceable." While I am saying this in jest, there is a ring of truth to the matter. You see, it is expensive to hire someone. More specifically, it is expensive to let someone leave. You have lost time and

---

1 Except about a million things my wife believes I've been wrong about.

2 Steve O'Brien. You should know this name. He has been an unbelievable lawyer, boss, corporate counsel, and mentor. I've stolen almost every one of these segment titles from words of wisdom that he has shared with me.

ghost work[3] when they go. You have lost productivity in the rumor mill of why they left. You have the obscene costs of recruitment with the Russian roulette risk of getting a bad replacement. After all that, you have to train and get the new, hopefully worthwhile, replacement employee up to speed.

But back to our story. This company had a large global presence. The funny thing about organizations like this is that in order to have a large global presence, you also need to have a lot of global offices, with a lot of global employees. That makes for global headaches. Not the least of which is the headache of opening an office to service clients in a foreign country and all of the red tape and paperwork that comes with not just the office, but also the red tape of hiring local nationals and the hard truth that immigration law isn't just a nightmare on a US Elm Street—it's also a global nightmare.

So, in the midst of all the global office openings and closings that this company was dealing with, there was a star employee. He was a rock star. Clients loved him. Coworkers wrote poems about him. He was destined to have his name written on the walls of the corporate hall of fame. Therefore, when the company needed to close an office in one European country due to some—*cough cough*—regulatory hiccups, the executive staff knew that losing this employee just wasn't in the cards.

So, they devised a very detailed and strategically sound plan. The legal team, believing this all to be true, and the executive team, also believing that said employee was worth moving mountains for, started a very long and expensive chain of events. They decided to move him to an office in another country. This country was more expensive, so pay would need to be adjusted. There would be increased visa and travel costs associated with moving him in and out of countries that weren't in the budget before. While everyone else in the soon-to-be-closed office was replaceable and could be fired, this employee was untouchable. No expense could be spared.

After months of planning, costs, and execution, it was time to shut the old company down and move this star employee to a neighboring country. There was only one problem. No one had thought to ask this future

---

3 Ghost work is the mountain of paperwork that sticks to a recently abandoned office when someone ghosts. They're gone, but the ghost of employee number 75534 haunts the old office like a plague. No one else will touch it, and no one really knows if it is important.

corporate hall of famer if that's what he wanted. You see where this is going. After the move, he quit. This company spent a boatload of cash and time, late nights, time zone-crossing phone calls, precious opportunity costs, and untold stress moving heaven and Earth to keep him, only to learn he didn't want to move.

How could this have happened? There was no evidence that this employee wanted to work anywhere else. How could everyone have been so completely blindsided? How could everyone have been so wrong?

Well, I think we all know the answer to that. It's easy to sit and judge from the outside. Truth be told, any one of us can make a similar mistake. We often can't believe our assumptions could ever be wrong. The problem is, they often are. We, as humans, often take the absence of evidence to mean evidence of an absence. We are wired to assume we are right and not to examine our assumptions.

This employee was a star. He was killing it. Beating the numbers, loved by all. Why wouldn't he stay and accept a move to a better office in a great country? This was a step up. Well, sometimes all it takes to make sure we aren't completely wrong is to understand it is possible, and to ask. In this case, it would have saved one company a lot of time and money.

You are a counsel. You are more than a lawyer. Be a counselor. Be sure to ask yourself if you could be wrong before giving counsel. Be especially sure when everyone agrees and it seems obvious. Those are the biggest screwups that often hurt the worst.

The Dump and Run

I love the holidays. For those not in the United States, I don't mean *all* holidays. I mean *THE* holidays. In the good old U S of A, that means basically the months of November and December. We start winding down for Thanksgiving around mid-November and don't really get back to working our butts off until well after the New Year's Eve hangover.

It used to be summer that everyone looked forward to. Trust me, that was before air-conditioning. Summer used to be so darn miserable in most of the country that nothing got done. Productivity tanked for all of July and August. No one could stand the heat in office buildings and factory floors. Work slowed to a crawl. Then the miracle of air-conditioning put a coffin full of nails into summer. Once everyone could work in a comfortable environment, long, lazy summers were over.

Now the only time that you can slow down is winter. And we were lucky enough to have some gracious Native Americans plan a dinner that morphed into Thanksgiving, and even luckier that it fell so close to Christmas. With those two major family holidays so close together, followed immediately by the New Year holiday, we get weeks on end of lower productivity and people taking more time for themselves and family. Oh, holy night.

That is, with the exception of highly responsible people on senior staff. That now includes you, in case you were wondering. You, my friend, get the benefit of being the recipient of the dump and run. It also happens on Fridays and on minor holidays, but it is especially aggravating when it happens on *The Holidays*.

You may already be familiar with a similar version of this from your law firm days. A senior partner or someone with some level of control over you walks in right before the end of the day or week and dumps a load of work on your desk and expects it back in the morning or after the weekend. They leave to enjoy their time off, and you do the work.

It is like that in corporate America too. There is a little bit of a difference. In your company, it won't be a boss who does this to you.[1] It will be an internal client. For now, let's take the example of a saleswoman. She will at some point walk into your office right before the holidays start and dump a mess of a deal on you. Then she will proceed to tell you that she is heading home for the holidays and won't be in cell range for a while. She needs to get back to the client soon, though, so please get to it as quickly as you can.

At this point, you will want to say no. You will wish you could shove all the paperwork right back onto her desk and tell her that the failure to plan ahead does not constitute an emergency on your part. You will, at least in your head, scream at her that it is your holiday, too, and that you have family you need to drive to go see. You'll even want to throw the B.S. flag on the idea that someone doesn't have cell reception anywhere in the world anymore.

You won't do any of that. You will find a way. You will think about the company, its sales goals, and your team. I know this because you won't get to the chair you will be sitting in by saying no or claiming it isn't your problem.

This will occur for as long as you let it. Don't get me wrong. It will always occur to some extent until the day you retire. The question is to what extent? It can be something that occasionally occurs with a few new people or bad apples. Or it could happen to you all the time by everyone in the company who sees you as a resource. That part is up to you.

There is a middle ground on the spectrum of the dump and run. On one end, you have Stage 1—getting walked on and abused. On the other end, you have Stage 10—screw you and this job. Neither of those is healthy

---

1 At least not all the time. If you aren't GC, it might happen occasionally.

or the right choice. Stage 5 is where you want to be. A corporate counsel at Stage 5 on the continuum is respected, appreciated, and is helping those in the organization work efficiently. He isn't saying no when a real issue arises that happens to fall right at the start of some needed time off, but he is setting correct expectations to assist everyone in knowing how to initiate workflow.

This isn't easy. It takes having courage to explain why dumping a load of work on your desk and running off for fun-time isn't acceptable. It also takes balancing that with your desire to be helpful and a tendency to self-sabotage. It takes time to train everyone that they need to prepare ahead. They need to let you know the expected workload so you can help them and still have a life.

This is important. If you end up sitting on a ton of work dropped on your desk the day before a holiday, don't say I didn't warn you. Set expectations now and prioritize. This will save your sanity and help you deliver top-notch legal service on the company's issues instead of working in a hurry over a holiday while everyone else is taking selfies by the fire and under the mistletoe with their families and friends.

The Calm Before the Storm: Use Time Wisely to Prepare for the Rough Times

If you are thinking *Duh!*, well, you aren't alone. I thought the same thing when my GC said it to me once. We all learned some version of this in kindergarten, and again in grade school, and if your dad was like mine, it was drilled into you. My ex-mother-in-law called it the six Ps—prior planning prevents piss-poor performance.

So if it is so clear, and if anyone who has made anything of themselves probably knows it, why is it in the survival guide? Good question. Because being in-house adds a wrinkle and whole other dimension to this mantra. I already talked about how hard it can be to weather the calm times, when your organization isn't in crisis mode. Well, now I'm giving you some ideas on how to do that.

There will be times when the business litigation dips to very low levels. Labor lawsuits are at a low tide, the government isn't subpoenaing you, your company isn't buying some other company or going through a reorg, and you just aren't under the gun at all. You will have two choices: You can catch up on your family life and see friends, even get a little done around the house, or you could dig into work, stay mentally engaged at the office, and look for weak spots. If you are really smart, you'll do both.

This is not an either/or scenario. These times are like gold. This isn't like when you worked at a law firm. When a big case settled or you finally got a verdict. At the firm, in the moments right after the gale-force winds pass you by, there is a massive high-pressure system that sits overhead with sunny skies and no waves.[1] You usually have to start looking for client work to bill against but are likely to take some time to actually see your husband or wife and maybe even check to make sure the children are still breathing.[2]

The one thing you won't be doing is looking for better ways to make your firm run, or looking to eliminate risk, or tighten your cyber defenses against a client PII breach. You have management committees and sub-committees for that. But in-house, this is the perfect time to look for real, meaningful ways to help your organization be a better managed, more efficient, and legally sound entity.

When we are buried in bet-the-company litigation, we're too busy to crash meetings we aren't invited to, which is a great risk-mitigation tool. We don't get the opportunity to just have coffee with colleagues and see what roadblocks the legal department needs to break through when every moment is taken on some other emergency matter.

When is the last time you really sat down with an internal client, over coffee and at your request, and asked them to tell you every way you make life harder for them? You'd be surprised how happy they will be to tell you just how many roadblocks they believe the legal department puts in front of their success. They'll be wrong on a lot of them, but if you avoid being defensive and really listen, you'll get some golden market research nuggets.

They will not only tell you how to help them, but you'll also gain mountains of internal efficiencies in the process. They might tell you about how long it is taking them to get nondisclosure agreements through the legal office, and they might complain that a contract with a big-fish client they have on the line is getting held up in long legal reviews. Ignore the instinct to point out all the reasons it takes that amount of time. Talk with them and let them help you find efficiencies to make your team's job go smoother and help speed up the process.

Once you are done having a series of one-on-one meetings with every internal client you can think of, it is time to start crashing meetings. This is going to come as a shock to the system for some people at first, so be very considerate and take the time to explain that you really are there just

---

1 Sorry about the nautical references. I'm a former Coastie and a lifelong sailor; the metaphors are just too good not to use.

2 We should all do that a little more than we do anyway. Just my two cents.

to help. Nobody, and I mean NOBODY, feels comfortable the first time some lawyer from the legal department invites herself to a meeting and just plops down and flips open a notebook.

Tell the person in advance that you might crash. Explain that you want to know more about what is going on with production, or sales, or whatever the meeting is about. Explain that you are only there to learn. Be careful about freaking out when they start spit-balling about their plans. You will hear no fewer than a hundred things in the first hour that make your skin crawl. Every idea they have will sound legally risky or downright crazy. If not, they are holding back out of fear that you're spying on them.

The goal is to listen, not to correct and tell them they are nuts. That is going to be so much harder than you realize right now. Don't say a word that isn't positive in those meetings.[3] You need to build trust. You aren't there to be the dream killer. Not yet. You have to realize that 99 percent of what they are talking about isn't going to happen anyway. They are being creative and trying ideas out on each other. Those risky plans have a lot of runway to them before they become reality. You have time to listen, learn, and slowly make suggestions that will prevent future headaches.

In all this time, you are building better systems. You are finding ways to deliver internal legal services more efficiently and tailored to your clients; you are looking for company risks to mitigate. These tasks seem like busywork, but they aren't. They are critical to surviving the times when an unforeseen storm hits you broadside. You won't have time for all of this when you're getting your butt handed to you. However, you might be a lot more efficient for all the groundwork you have done. It will save you valuable time and headaches and allow you to thrive in the crisis and serve your client.

As for the family, the house chores, and the dog. Make sure you strengthen those items as well. Your family and friends are an invaluable support system when times are tough. When things are running smooth, bring home the easy work and watch a movie with your partner. Take the easy work on a long weekend with the kids. You don't need to be in the office twelve hours a day during the easy times. You can take this advice for what it's worth. I know it has helped me more than I can describe.

---

3 Caveat. If they seem hell-bent on criminal activity. You need to do something fast. Chances are, you'll never be in a meeting where someone suggests outright criminal activity, but if they do, you better do something.

There's No Time Like Now

I happen to be writing this in the early part of the year. I will go to the gym for lunch, as I do almost every day of every year, and instead of having my pick of machines, weights, and spin bikes, I will have to wait and feel crowded. That's because my gym will be inundated with people who wait until January first of every year to realize they fell off the exercise bandwagon ten months ago and now have to get into shape.

It's horrible. Have you ever had to stand in line with a bunch of sweaty people waiting on a shower? I didn't mind it so much in the military, but I'm paying for this. Every year in January I stand there barefoot and exposed after my workouts. I do this while all of us stand in a line resembling my parochial school formation between classes, less the uniform—or any clothes, for that matter.

Do you know what goes through my head during this mildly awful experience? It isn't that I wish these guys weren't crowding my gym space. It is that I wish they would just show up all year so we could build more shower stalls to accommodate everyone, and I wouldn't have to deal with this every New Year.

It also makes me think about work, and life, and all the other things that people, including me, sometimes put off until we just can't put them off any longer. Why in the world do we do this?

Most of the problems that build up on our desks or in our in-boxes are a result of one simple problem. We simply don't show up all year. I don't mean that in the literal sense, of course. I mean it in the metaphorical way. Some people can't help but phone it in. We are present but not really all there.

This train of thought somehow got me thinking about bonuses. At a firm, the bonus is really about hours. If you hit your hours, and everyone else pretty much hits theirs as well, the firm should be pretty profitable, and as a result there will be a tier of bonuses based on either seniority or production of billables.

That doesn't really work inside a company. That is not how bonuses work, and if you asked for a bonus for internally billing your own company more time, they have a perverse incentive to actually work with you as much as they should. This is all irrelevant, since your bonus will be set by the company and industry you work for anyway.

When you first start interviewing for in-house jobs, the idea of trying to negotiate how much of your pay is in salary and how much is in bonus is a little tricky. How you are being measured for that bonus isn't as mathematically simple as, "Bill over 2,400 hours and get the market bonus as long as the firm hits X revenue per partner."

Some companies do bonuses on stock performance and some on earnings or revenue goals. But with so many different divisions having so many different missions within the organization, the bonus of a director in production might vary 180 degrees from the bonus structure of a first-year business development associate. The lawyers aren't any different.

It might seem like I'm getting ready to give you bonus-negotiation strategy, which would be odd considering where we started. I'm not. What I am going to tell you is that however your bonus is decided, there is one thing that is common for every lawyer at a firm, every director in the production division, and every salesperson.

Bonuses aren't decided right at bonus time. They are decided in the little moments that you don't phone it in. They are accrued when you and your team put in just a little extra effort on every detail. They get bigger when you don't quit hitting it hard in March but stick to the mental gym of your office all year long.

You will become bedrock in the foundation of your company. You will mitigate risk, give strategic advice, prevent mishaps, and fight in the trenches to minimize damage when something goes wrong. All of this will lead to a larger earnings per share and a larger slice of the pie for you at bonus time.

As to the bonus negotiation, that part is a lot easier. Find some market research and ask for something similar to what the best of your profession in your industry are being paid. Then go earn it.

AVOID THE LAND MINES

Zugzwang

It's a lot like schadenfreude,[1] but better. There is a moment when the other side knows they can't win. They have been outplayed, outmaneuvered, and outgunned. You'll notice it, ever so briefly sometimes or more obviously in others. It will show up in their eyes. It's that moment they know they have been beaten. Totally and utterly laid bare and beaten. Do not revel in this moment. It is at this moment when people are dangerous and unpredictable.

If you have competition as a leading strength,[2] you can't help but live for the battle and revel in the win. Like me, you can't look for enough things to compete in. You race to the water fountain, see if you can do anything faster or better than everyone else, and just plain love a good race. But you have to manage your strengths. You can't just let them run wild. When you have someone in a position of zugzwang, manage this strength with all your might.

Use other strengths in your arsenal, like discipline and responsibility. You owe it to your team and to your client to not let your competitive juices turn a cornered adversary into a raging beast. You will still win, but

---

1 No, it isn't. Just because it's German and sounds funny doesn't make them the same, geesh.

2 I have competition as my number four strength on the Clifton StrengthsFinder Assessment. If you don't know your strengths, you're missing out on valuable information about yourself that can really help you grow as a leader and a lawyer.

the damage will not be contained. An opponent in zugzwang will go out quietly if allowed to with grace or will burn everything to the ground if not given an opportunity to save face. That isn't a win for your client. It also isn't being a good human being. Try this, even when the opponent seems bound and determined to make it hard for you.

I have a close friend who advanced through a large Fortune 50 firm quite rapidly. He went from being an unknown business analyst to a junior executive and vice president in charge of all government relations at an age when his peers with whom he was hired had just barely eked out their first promotions. You don't do that without beating a few adversaries and taking a few jobs from more senior executives. This can be done graciously. It must. It also doesn't just happen on the business side of the house. It happens on legal teams and it happens in external matters with opposing counsel.

People don't just go away after they have been vanquished. They still exist, and they remember if you won fairly and if you won with humility. One of the final people my friend overcame in his quest for the brass ring was an accomplished veteran of the legal/government relations game. She had much more experience, but my friend took a job she was sure was hers. She all but had her business cards printed and the nameplate engraved and ready for the corner office.

It didn't work out that way. My friend got the role, and she lost her job. When her zugzwang moment happened, she was a cornered adversary. He didn't gloat, he didn't twist the knife, and he didn't seek revenge for the months of angling she had done in her own quest for the role. He acted with grace and humility.

It turned out to be a good move. She didn't just disappear, but she also found another position in the industry. Can you imagine the cold dish of revenge that would have been served upon my friend and his company in matters involving Congress if personal vendettas were at hand? Allowing someone to lose with honor will allow you to run into them professionally in the future without the fear of irrational flame throwing that would ultimately hurt your company. Don't let it happen.

It isn't just after-the-fact issues either. An opponent is most dangerous while still in the zugzwang. I will never forget one litigation matter that was nearing completion. Our side had flown to another city to negotiate a settlement with the opposing side. After a brief hello, the attorney for the other company made some pretty inaccurate statements about disputed facts and then asked for the moon. It was pretty clear we weren't as near a settlement as both sides believed, so we left. Ten minutes, start to finish. They made opening discussion statements and made a demand; we got up and walked out.

That started the next round in this brass-knuckled litigation. I prepared for trial. After that conference, I prepared for it to go all the way. I left no stone unturned and lined up a host of international discovery. It was time to go all the way and I wanted to be prepared for a sure win. At some point, the other side realized that this was not going to end well. They, and especially the opposing trial lawyer, saw the writing on the wall and started calling me for a settlement. Remembering our last discussion, I politely said no and that we'd rather try the case.

A very wise boss took a call from a very senior attorney from the other side who wanted to know whether I had lost my mind. Was I really going to corner their trial counsel and their client, who were both now hell-bent on burning everything to the ground instead of going for a very cheap settlement? I was. I wasn't going to let them lose graciously. I was going to go all in and make their client suffer. Thankfully, I had a mentor and boss who wasn't going to let that happen.

When you have someone on the ropes, when they are begging to end it, end it. Take yes for an answer. Allow a defeated opponent a way out. Don't make a permanent enemy. Don't force a cornered and wounded foe to burn it all to the ground.

Revenge Is a Dish Best Served Cold

We all need a little motivation. Some of us thrive on the daily competition of litigation, or any other matter we worked as outside counsel with an adversary. It can be hard to motivate oneself when that goes away. Competition is a strength that motivates most lawyers I know. In place of that, revenge can be a great motivator.[1]

Some people seem to be able to bill an unlimited amount of hours. They have the innate ability to work on a matter or an issue until its very conclusion without any lack of motivation. Others need something else to keep motivated. One thing I have realized is that no one will work harder than when they really want to stick it to someone.

There are numerous reasons, any one of which are perfectly acceptable and will make great motivators. It may be just that the other party, or even the lawyer on the other side of this issue, has repeatedly done something you just can't agree with as a matter of principle. Stick it to them—find your inner revenge.[2] Sometimes it isn't a person but an institution that can

---

1 See the earlier chapter on not making enemies. Don't give them the same motivation.

2 Keep in mind the other survival tips. You owe it to your client to keep their best interests at the forefront. Use revenge for motivation but don't let it cloud your judgment.

drive you to work a case or a matter to the point that no other reasonable person would have.

I will attempt to give you two good examples. The first one happened to me and the second to a friend. The point is the same and the fact pattern quite similar.

I was working a business litigation matter. It wasn't personal, just business. Even though it wasn't *bet-the-company* in terms of size, it had some reputational issues at stake due mostly to the players. I decided to try this one in-house, rather than to farm it out.[3] The other organization was represented by quite competent counsel from a major firm. The lawyers on the case both went to a Top 14 (T14) law school. I did not. I went at night while serving on active duty and still have more than a little chip on my shoulder when confronted with lawyers who went to a T14.

So I did what any self-respecting lawyer would. I treated the opposing counsel as the face of every kid who had the luxury of going straight from undergrad to a highly ranked law school without working or having a family to worry about. I made working that case my sole life mission. If I didn't have time, I just worked overnight and through the weekend. I read every document three times. I put more hours into that case than any lawyer with half a brain would have.

Why? Revenge. I couldn't stand the idea of being beaten by either of the lawyers on the other side. I wanted them to know just how little I thought of the difference in education a T14 school meant. I wanted them to know that they weren't just going to be beaten—they would be soundly beaten by someone who attended, what in my mind I thought them to believe, an inferior school. Revenge.

This wasn't all too different from a story of a close friend of mine. He had applied to Harvard Law and was given the nicest of rejection letters. While he knew that Harvard was a long shot, the feeling of being rejected still stung. So what did our hero lawyer do later in practice? He took that rejection out on every Harvard-trained lawyer he ever came across in the rest of his practice.[4] And I do mean every time.

---

3 Well, I begged and my boss graciously permitted it. "I decided" just has a better ring to it.

4 Not literally, metaphorically.

God help the poor Harvard Law sap who happened to draw a case or matter that my friend ended up on the other side of. He wouldn't rest until he wiped the floor with them. It was his coup de grâce, his waterloo, and the hill he would die on every time if need be. There weren't enough hours in any day to hold the amount of time and resources he would throw into obliterating the other side if they made the mistake of hiring a Harvard Law alum for their counsel.

Funny thing, though, is I think he even did this on matters where the Harvard man or woman was working on the same side. He would still outwork them every day and twice on Sunday. It was a matter of pride. Harvard just didn't know what they missed out on. He was bound and determined to prove it. Revenge. The great motivator beyond all others.

When Times Are Tough and Sales Goals Are Coming Due, Salespeople Will Sell Roadkill and Call It a Fish

Maybe I should start this with a little explanation. One of my employers had a way of referring to a deal. It was a fish. Sometimes the fish got away, and people would tell Moby Dick–sized tales of how big it was going to be and how it just barely broke the line. Sometimes they would land the fish, and it would smell rotten within the first month of the project. And sometimes it wasn't a fish at all. It was roadkill dressed up in a fish Halloween costume.

You usually see this when the pressure is on. Companies need to make revenue numbers, so they put pressure on the sales line leads. The line leads put pressure on the middle managers. The middle . . . you get the point. Some saleswoman needs to make quota. She is tired of her bait getting stripped off her line, so on the way back to the truck from her fishing spot, she scoops up some roadkill in the parking lot and drags it back home to clean and cook.[1]

You might be asking yourself, "What the heck does this have to do with me and my department?" Well, everything. Your job is to keep the company safe. And a diet of roadkill is bad for the gut. It'll make your organization sick. It is not a nutritious and sustainable diet. Your job, if you are doing it right, is to stand at the door to the kitchen and stop them from bringing in roadkill that is disguised as a fish.

---

1 Okay. You're right. I took this metaphor a little too far.

Trust me, it will be disguised. No one brings a deal home that smells like rotting possum. They doctor it up a little first. They tell themselves that it's a great deal. They use key language that fits the organization and masks the deal as a garden-variety sale. Otherwise, the company would need an eagle eye like you to spot it and throw it back on the road where it belongs.

In order to do this, you need to be involved early and heavily. You can't know a bad deal if you don't know the components of a good one. That means knowing your organization and its services and products. You need to know the rights usually transferred, the changes the organization is willing to make to its standard offerings, the personnel usually used,[2] and the timelines that will make or break a successful project.

Then you need to know what is going on financially within your organization. I know it is a joke that lawyers go to law school because they hate numbers. Too bad. You need to be able to spot trends and see when the pressure is going to rise before the pressure rises. This will allow you to inject yourself more into the daily meetings and get a sense for what is in the pipeline. Without doing this, you'll be behind the eight ball. You'll have no visual on the problem areas. Look at year-to-date sales goals. Watch the revenue line, but also watch the gross earnings line. It will give you a way to see the hidden pressure that builds when revenue looks healthy but the organization is bleeding cash in costs.

When you see key metrics trending toward a pressure for future fast deals, start looking out for dead animals dressed up as fish. You'll smell them coming long before anyone else. But then you need to do something about it.

First, let the teams know that you know they are feeling pressure. Remind them of what a healthy deal looks like. Remind them of the goals for profitable projects, within the experience of the organization, won ethically. Let them know you are watching and are there to help them. You aren't the sales prevention department. Just knowing you are aware and watching will prevent a lot of this problem.

Next, you need to review deals that have the potential for organizational exposure. This isn't just reviewing the legal terms and ignoring the statements of work. It involves maintaining a core team of contract

---

2 This is called a staffing plan.

management professionals to review closed deals with you to ensure that pricing aligns with the organization's policies, that IT requirements aren't beyond your ability, and that the staffing plans and deadlines can be met.

You better be wary of any deal that looks like something outside the organization's normal wheelhouse. It's okay to grow and stretch, but it should be done strategically. This isn't something to be done at the whim of a desperate salesperson. They are often looking at the short-term goal of their bonus check. You have to worry about the long-term effects of taking on work that will lose money and risk your company's reputation.

And that leads us to the hardest part. Exposing the roadkill for what it is. Or better yet, what it isn't—a fish. That means some short-term pain. Sending the salesperson back to the negotiation table to reopen a "closed" deal. Fighting for better numbers, longer timelines, less restrictive IT security policies, or any number of items that clean the stink off the deal.

This won't be fun, but it's your job. Do it well.

Get Off My Lawn!

My hope is that you read that intro line in the grumpiest, old man of voices and conjured up an image of pants too high, suspenders, and lots of wrinkles.

We tend to think of people who yell something like this at kids cutting through the neighborhood as old curmudgeons. I mean, in some ways, they are. That's why I am almost sure that the image I described is what came to your mind as you read "Get off my lawn!"

But don't they have a point? I mean, it's their lawn. They bought it, they maintain it, they own it, and they care for it. They have to replace any damage you do to it while carelessly and illegally stomping all over it. While you're on it, they don't have the ability to use it 100 percent in the manner they want, even if all they want is to look at it without some punk kid on the grass.

There is one thing that almost every company in the world shares with the old man hero of the lawn. Every company has a lawn of intellectual property, and the world's punk neighbor kids are stomping all over it. I admit it, even I've been that punk kid.

I had the first Internet connection in my frat house. Do you know what I did with that Internet connection? I stole a boatload of music. I downloaded every song I could think of, and more than enough viruses too. At the time, I was a dumb kid. I grew up sharing music. We copied songs off the radio on tape and when CDs came around, we copied those and shared them too.

I just didn't view it as stealing. I had no idea I was participating in the downfall of the music industry as I knew it. Artists would suffer, record labels would suffer,[1] and record stores would close. Going to Vintage Vinyl in St. Louis and putting on a record, CD, or tape in the sound booths was one of my favorite things, and I was blindly aiding in the entire industry's downfall.

When the Recording Industry Association of America started suing people for piracy and Napster got kneecapped, I was furious. How dare they tell me to get off their lawn? I had every right to share my music with anyone I wanted and they should be able to share it with me, right?

Well, the problem is now considerably worse. We are losing untold revenue to piracy. Some of it is obvious. All digitally recorded entertainment is basically up for grabs by people who don't care. They rationalize it in a lot of ways. They say the artists and actors are overpaid. They say the ticket prices and song costs are too high. They somehow deserve the entertainment for free.

This sucks the lifeblood from the industries that do the research and development for new products, robs artists and distribution channels of revenue to continue providing the products, and ultimately devastates the pipeline of things that the thieves so desperately want.

It is taking place on a mass scale. Fake designer products for sale online. Even fake, and often unsafe, bike components that sell for thousands of dollars.

As a corporate counsel, you have your work cut out for you. This is way beyond dusting off a cease-and-desist letter every now and then. You will be playing Whac-A-Mole with IP thieves and counterfeiters. They will attempt to steal your company blind. They will do it in your company's home language and in every foreign language you can imagine.

You have to make this a priority from the very start. Fake goods and services diminish your revenue, but they also cheapen your brand. No IP thief copies you and does a better job at quality control. They don't care about your reputation. They are stealing it.

---

1 I know. It's hard to feel bad for record labels that were screwing over artists, but that's beside the point.

So from day one, make this a priority. It isn't your most pressing issue, at least not usually, but it is an omnipresent problem lurking in the background. Can you imagine litigating a case for a product defect, sinking a ton of money in discovery, only to realize when your expert witness is testing the evidence that it wasn't made by you at all? Worse yet, imagine the copy is so good your expert doesn't notice that it is an impostor, and your company is on the hook for a manufacturing defect you didn't even cause.

If you let things go that far, you've waited too long. Have a long-term strategy for fighting off the neighborhood punks. It's your lawn; they have no right to cut across it.

Salespeople Are Bred Not to Take No for an Answer. Great for Sales, Not So Much for Compliance

Salespeople. They really are something else. You need them; your company needs them. Without them you don't even have a job. Who else is going to bring in all of that cash? It doesn't make sense to get upset at salespeople for making a lot of money. I hate it when I see people in the back office who get jealous of salespeople with a nice car or with the flashy watch. Salespeople are the lifeblood of the organization.

It takes a rare breed to make a good salesperson. They just won't take no for an answer—at least not the successful ones. I don't know about you, but I'm not keen on getting hung up on every day. I'm not keen on getting a phone slammed in my ear or a door shut in my face. That is essentially what a salesperson puts up with almost every day. The good ones take it on the chin over and over and over again.

If they are really good, then they will make your organization a ton of money because they will do this with a smile. They know that with every one of those hang-ups, for every one of those doors slammed in their face, there is a sale waiting to be made. These poor guys just won't take no for an answer.

This is the very essence of what makes them great at sales and horrible at compliance. What is hard is accepting this. You can't get mad at them for being who they are. It is in their DNA. If they weren't hardheaded and always looking for an angle or looking for a way to get something done, they wouldn't be in sales. At least, they wouldn't be any good at it. It turns out that it is really, really difficult for them to switch that mentality off when it comes to complying with your company's code of conduct or chosen ethics.

So what are you supposed to do? How do you deal with having someone who needs to have a certain level of stubbornness when it comes to driving profitability for the company and still make sure they're willing to listen to you and follow the law as well as your company's values? Well, we could write an entire book on corporate compliance programs, but that isn't the point of this book. Most of you are not going to be your company's chief of corporate compliance as well as a GC. So how do you do the little things, short of revamping the entire compliance program, that will get your salespeople to stop acting like salespeople when they're dealing with the things that put the company at risk?

For one thing, you have to stop beating your head into the wall. You have to stop trying to change them and getting frustrated. It won't work. They won't be changed. Realize who they are and play to their strengths. You're a lawyer, and you should be at least somewhat adept at reading people and making arguments that help to persuade them. If not, you really need to check how you got this job.

You can start off by convincing them you aren't the sales-prevention department. This will go a long way in establishing some trust. They want to know that they can come to you and help get deals closed. They don't want to know about the obstacles. They want to hear solutions. If you need to let them know that there is a significant compliance barrier to a deal, have a solution ready. These people aren't used to hearing no and just stopping. They won't do it. If you don't have an alternative way to get the deal closed, they will just find a way to ignore you. That puts everyone at risk.

At some point in your career you will have a Bob. Everyone has a Bob. My Bob was an unbelievable salesperson. A real rainmaker. Unfortunately, he almost never took no for an answer. Great for sales, hard to manage. Bob never wanted to hear that he couldn't get a deal closed. It didn't matter what the obstacle was. If the other side was willing to sign, he needed legal to find a way to make it work.

Bob would sit in my office and argue until he was blue in the face. "Because it's illegal" wasn't a good enough answer for him. You better be prepared to show him why it was illegal, what statute was saying it was illegal, and how you could do the same thing and make it legal. He would argue the nuance of every regulation, every clause in a contract, and every line of code from the Code of Federal Regulations. He just wouldn't take no for an answer.

But do you know the funny thing about Bob? He made me a better lawyer. He made my contracts manager a superior professional who was much better at her job. Both of us knew that if we had to tell Bob no, then we couldn't be lazy about it. We had to come to that conversation prepared. We had to know exactly why we believed that it wouldn't be compliant or wouldn't be legal to do things the way he wanted to do them. And then we better darn well have a better solution to help him get the deal done.

This used to drive my contract manager crazy. She couldn't understand why he wouldn't just take no for an answer or listen when we told him that something wasn't going to work. Only when she became a shareholder in the company did it really sink in. You want these people to not take no for an answer. The company needs them to refuse to hear no.

In the end, the most important thing is to manage them closely, manage them well, and keep an eye on them. Be prepared for every conversation, and in the end, if they actually don't take your advice and put the company at risk, ask yourself if it was their fault or yours. If it was theirs and they blatantly disregarded your advice, they need to go no matter how much they sell. But be careful not to just jump to that conclusion. If you were too lazy to work with a good salesperson who wouldn't hear no for an answer, you need to evaluate how you deal with a rainmaker.

DOJ Gets Real Ticked at a Hold Order Gone Wrong

There are a few things that really get under the skin of the lawyers at the Department of Justice. One of the big ones is screwing up a hold order.

In the olden timey days, when documents were actual pieces of paper in real, tangible file cabinets, document holds were pretty easy.[1] You went to the document custodian, usually the file room clerk or the person who had the keys to the file room or file cabinet, and you handed them a hold order that stated you'd personally hunt them down if they let documents out of their sight that might in any way be responsive to a list of things relating to some pending litigation matter.

We aren't in the olden timey days. Today, documents live in the Interwebs and might be printed and in the office of God only knows how many potential custodians. When ABC News put out a story in 2002 that Enron destroyed documents "by the truckload," and the markets collapsed in a wave of corporate accounting failures, the DOJ, Congress, and the SEC took notice.

Sarbanes Oxley was passed in 2002, and the SEC in 2003 released its final rule on the retention of records relevant to audits and reviews. As the final rule discussed, "Section 802 of the Sarbanes-Oxley Act is intended

---

1 At least that is what I've been told by the lawyers with even more gray hair than me.

to address the *destruction or fabrication of evidence and the preservation* of 'financial and audit records.'"

Congress got in on the act as well, passing 18 U.S.C. § 1519. Whoever knowingly alters, destroys, mutilates, conceals, covers up, falsifies, or makes a false entry in any record, document, or tangible object with the intent to impede, obstruct, or influence the investigation or proper administration of any matter within the jurisdiction of any department or agency of the United States or any case filed under title 11, or in relation to or contemplation of any such matter or case, shall be fined under this title, imprisoned not more than twenty years, or both.

It seemed as though this new power would sit dormant, until about 2010. The feds tried it out first on executives from the Wolff Company, a global supplier of honey and German food products. It seems they deleted a host of e-mails and chats about their illegal honey sourcing scheme.[2]

Seven years later, and we are watching an implosion of a different German-based company. This one makes automobiles. Evidently, they lied, a lot, about how clean their diesel engines could run. Turns out, they weren't clean. They were big polluting machines running software to trick the government testers.

Well, about six executives thus far are now charged with felonies. One, a senior compliance officer, got locked up while vacationing in Miami. You know who is currently, as I write this, an unindicted coconspirator? A lawyer. The in-house counsel who royally screwed the pooch on the document hold. Do you know what "unindicted coconspirator" means? It means "guy who is probably about to lose his law license and go to jail." In DOJ speak, it means we are still investigating you, and you're one of the big fish we intend to fry.[3] It means they are going to tar and feather him, and beat the heck out of him in the most public of ways.

Do you know what our in-house contemporary did to deserve such public lashings? He is accused of tipping off the other guys that a hold order might be coming soon, so if there were any loose documents admitting

---

2 Honey. A ton of illegal honey comes from China. I was a little shocked to learn that unless I was buying honey VERY locally, I was almost assuredly buying watered down fake and mislabeled Chinese honey. Who knew?

3 With Old Bay seasoning. All fish is better with Old Bay.

to corporate malfeasance, better to shred them now because once a hold order was issued, it would be too late.

Now all this might be overblown. He might be innocent. Heck, maybe they all are. So far, there hasn't been a trial outside of the one in the *Wall Street Journal* Compliance section. Let's face it, the media trial doesn't always have all the facts that end up in the real trial.

There will be all kinds of fancy software to help you adequately do a document hold. But that won't actually help you as much as you wish. Software isn't a magic bullet. Systems are the thing that prevents you from becoming the next "unindicted coconspirator."

What systems, you ask? Have a plan in place for how you will handle document retention before situations and litigation arise. Follow that plan in a reasonable manner, and then document what you did. Don't tell anyone about your intention to issue a hold order with time for them to destroy things. This tends to be viewed by enforcement authorities as a "tip-off."

Defend your company based on the facts. The facts are in the documents, and it is your job to protect those documents. It won't be fun, but it is ethical, it's mandated by law, and it will keep you out of jail.

Let's Play the Game of Risk

In business, there is an indefinite, limitless amount of risk. There is risk everywhere. Employee litigation risk, environmental risk to your facilities, risk of IT infrastructure breach, risk of competitor innovation, and a metric ton[1] of legal risk.

Different organizations have different risk appetites. Not everyone looks at all legal and business risk with the same level of care, and not everyone or every organization takes on as much risk as they potentially could. This is not as linear as you might expect. A novice might expect all organizations to follow a risk graph that resembles something like this:

---

[1] I'm not sure if a metric ton is bigger than a good old-fashioned American ton, but it sounds bigger.

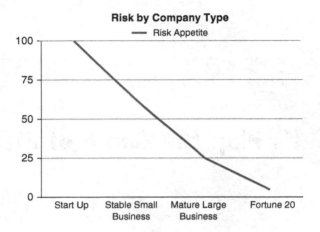

The above assumed risk tolerance chart seems right. It feels right intuitively. The young start-up takes on a ton of legal and business risk. It has to be agile, nimble, and might not have enough personnel with knowledge to even realize the risk they are taking on. Contrast that with the Fortune 20, blue chip firm that has everything to lose.

But not all enterprises are going to fit this mold. You have to anticipate that you could walk into a start-up as the new GC and find a group of investors who don't want to make a single decision without knowing with 100 percent certainty that they have avoided all risk.[2] You also might work as a senior counsel at a Fortune 20 that isn't old at all; has shot up in size through sheer luck, timing, and smart acquisitions; and is the risk equivalent of a child running with scissors.

Why will this matter to you as a new in-house counsel? You are going to be a key stakeholder in helping your organization walk a tightrope. You have to be able to accurately assess how much risk management wants to accept and give advice that balances that risk tolerance with a need for growth.

Anyone can prevent a risky situation from happening. But if that risk-avoidance strategy equals zero growth—or worse, negative growth— the organization has failed at its mission.

I'll give you an analogy from the IT space. Technology needs to serve some purpose. I can give you an absolutely secure PC or laptop. All you

---

2 This start-up is going to have a rough go. Just sayin'.

have to do is never turn it on, hook up a single device to it, and definitely not hook it up to the Internet. In other words, don't use it for its intended purpose. See below for a pretty accurate visualization of the inverse relationship between security/risk avoidance and effectiveness.

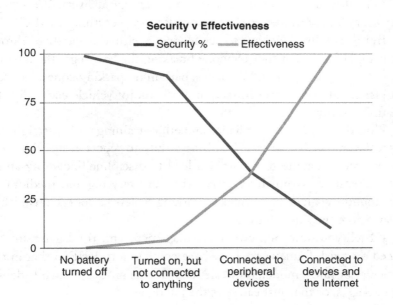

This is where you come in. You have to help your organization make the hard decisions about how much risk they want to tolerate while still making sales. They can't have absolute security and unlimited growth potential. You need to help them mitigate risks while gaining shareholder value.

There are several schools of thought on risk and growth. One I will call the "Uber" risk model. In this model, you act like a start-up no matter how large or small your organization is. You take on huge amounts of risk, knowing that you will make some "parking ticket" infractions of regulations along the way, but you grow anyway. You pay the fines as you lose the cases over your infractions, but you never stymie growth in the process.

There is a big internal risk to your organization with this model. It is very hard to manage your internal communications around compliance and ethics while admitting you aren't going to follow every law—on purpose.

Think about the overnight package delivery business.[3] The business model of delivering packages in tight urban environments relies on breaking the parking and traffic laws of every city they operate in. If you were to ask them, you would get this reply on fancy corporate letterhead:

"Thank you for your inquiry to XYZ package delivery. We strive to obey every law, both in spirit and in practice, in everything we do."

But internally, they have to acknowledge, either explicitly or through not firing drivers, that they condone breaking the law to get the job done. They double park, park in bike lanes, park in no parking zones, and commit just about every other infraction of the motor vehicle code, all before I've finished my first cup of coffee.

How do they hold compliance and ethics training with a straight face, when the trainer has to say, "You have a duty to report every violation of law or policy? Failure to report will lead to discipline, including and up to termination." Meanwhile, every driver in every big and medium-size city around the globe has a stack of parking tickets under each windshield wiper before the sun is fully risen.

I'll tell you how. Somewhere, management and the legal team have agreed on a risk framework. They have come to a realization that in their particular business model, they can't obey traffic ordinances while delivering packages, or they just can't get the job done.

They probably had a conversation that covered the finer points of the difference between ordinances and regulations that have no basis in ethics and those that are truly ethical in nature, and have made the decision that some of the ones that are purely regulatory but lacking any ethics basis just have to be ignored and the fines paid.

This might seem cynical and hard for some people to get their head around, but you're going to run into this at some point in your career in-house. Everyone knows, even four-year-olds, that stealing, killing, and hitting people is wrong. A four-year-old has no concept of only parking in the delivery zone between the hours of 7:00 a.m. to 3:00 p.m. as a matter of right and wrong. It is just one of those rules that keeps the regulatory state afloat and maintains order to our lives but sometimes doesn't fit neatly into getting real-world work done.

---

3 These guys usually drive solid brown or white trucks, but they shall remain nameless.

That is the uncomfortable space that you will find yourself navigating with the board and your executive team. They need your counsel in advising them on how to get real-world work done while balancing the need to be a good corporate citizen.

I used Uber as an example because in my opinion, this risk model relies on rapid expansion in regulatory gray areas. It counts on finding so many customers in any one area that the regulators are forced to either bend the regulations to the company's business model or have their own constituents freak out on them when they regulate the company out of operation in their area.

In this model, sometimes you lose. Come to find out, the people are willing to go back to a second-rate form of transport like a taxi without so much as a single tweet of angst at the taxi commissioner for over-regulating you out of work. You end up with a huge fine and potentially workers or contractors facing legal action.

You might be the one called on to help your company make this call, and it won't be easy. This will be especially true if you are risk averse[4] and are used to being able to say, "Do X, because there is a law or regulation against doing Y."

But the opposite might also be true. You might be the one who has to get the management team to turn on the proverbial computer and plug it into the wall. Otherwise the company, like a shut-down computer, is useless. It stops taking all risk or takes so long trying to mitigate every risk that it gets beat to market every time by its competitors.

Allowing a company to do this while you are its lawyer is just as bad as allowing them to run with scissors. Either one of these outcomes is likely to have our tightrope-walking man fall to his death. The company either slips and dies from a lack of ability to take the risk and move forward, or it slips to its death from taking too much risk without a care for how far the fall.

Set up a risk chart, talk about the likelihood of scenarios and the risk to the overall health of the organization if there is a failure, and give your honest advice of how likely that failure is to occur. Then grow some thick skin and make a recommendation. Let them know you understand the risk tolerance DNA, have evaluated the risks and opportunities, and have their back. It's ultimately their decision, but they need your advice to make it.

---

4 Face it. All lawyers are a little risk averse. We see laws, statutes, and potential torts everywhere.

THE BUSINESS OF LAW IN A BUSINESS

There Is More to a Legal Matter Than Just Winning

Everyone looks at issues through the prism of their own experiences. As outside counsel, I often viewed things on my desk as tasks to "win" at. Some of this is just because I like to compete. A lot of it is just my way of looking at the issue.

My clients weren't always looking at it the same way. This wasn't a game, and it wasn't something to "win." It was a life matter that had real-world consequences. They wanted their life back to normal, and they wanted the headache over.

Litigation has a way of messing up all the little things that need to occur for a business. Corporate designee depos have a real business impact. Think of all the things your chief information officer (CIO) could be doing for your company if she wasn't stuck in depo prep, and then a deposition, and then worrying about how she did in her deposition.

Litigation is hugely unproductive for a company. It is a distraction at best and a PR nightmare leading to state attorney general investigations at its worst.

The hourly billing model has always had an ill side effect of putting at least one of the outside counsel's interests against that of the company client. The financial incentive for a litigation matter to last forever can't be ignored, even if I do believe that almost all good outside counsel are ethical at their core and don't intentionally draw out a matter. You still can't ignore that the conflict exists.

All of these issues get to the heart of one of the most important things you'll do as an in-house attorney when managing outside counsel handling a litigation matter. You need to be prepared to evaluate a case early and decide just how much interruption to your core business is worth it. Then you have to be open and frank with outside counsel about that belief.

This should seem obvious, but depending on where you work, it may be harder than you think. While we like to believe that business litigation is "just business," the people who run companies are still people. They aren't robots. They have feelings, and those feelings get really hurt.

Getting to the executive committee early with a cold, hard diagnosis of the business impact of protracted litigation weighed against potential impacts can be sobering and bring even the most emotional CFO around to understanding when to go to the mattresses and when to call off the dogs.

The even more difficult task is talking your outside counsel out of the mind-set that every motion must be won, every deponent destroyed. That isn't always the path to the best outcome. Treating a wounded and heartbroken widow of a defective product explosion in a manufacturing defect case harshly and without compassion isn't always going to lead you to your real best outcome. Destroying her on the stand or in a deposition is a temporary win that might cost the battle. This example seems clear, but they aren't always so in-your-face obvious.

Ask yourself early: What's a case worth? What is the business disruption? And what's the path of least resistance to get the best outcome with the least damage to business operations? It's a simple thing to ask yourself at the very beginning of a matter that might save you and your company a lot of money and angst in the long run.

Buying Company Stock: Be Prepared to Be an Owner

You are going to be an owner of a corporation. Well, at least most of you will. It is inevitable. This isn't much different than making partner at a firm. At some point, the company will come to you and let you know it is time to buy in. Be ready for it.

This might be great, or it might happen at a point in your life when you just can't swing dropping a lot of coin on your employer's stock, a stock that may or may not be a good buy. Employee stock plans come in a wide variety of sizes and shapes. You might get some stock as a part of your pay package. Maybe you get options. Maybe you get none of that, but you will get an opportunity to buy in.

This is a potential minefield for you. Can you imagine being at your firm, being offered partner, and saying, "No thanks, but I'll keep collecting a check. I'm just not all that into being fully invested in this firm's future." Well, if you turn down a stock buy when offered, that's what you are telling your company. You are thought of as a leader. General counsels have slowly morphed into a serious leadership role in their organizations. Most of those organizations now expect a level of commitment and "ownership" of their counsel.

Some of you will be lucky. There will be a pretty clear plan in place that will tell you exactly what is on senior management's mind when it comes to the amount of stock you "should" own. For the rest of you, this is dangerous territory. Hopefully, by the time you are invited to buy in, you will have close friends in the organization who are senior enough to have already been down this road. They might be able to light your path.

The danger is that you either buy too little, which doesn't show much commitment to your company and belief in its future, or you buy way more than you need to, and you end up drastically overexposed financially to one investment.[1] Either one puts your future at risk.

So what's the right amount? Well, depending on what level you are in the organization, it can be a pretty grand sum of money, and it will definitely conflict with your financial advisor's advice on not putting so many eggs in one basket. For illustration, I'll give you a pretty standard table based on a banking or service industry stock ownership guideline. The multiple is the amount you need in terms of your yearly salary.

Multiple	Position
6x	Chairman and CEO
4x	Executive vice chairman and president
3x	CFO, executive vice presidents & executive management committee
2x	Other executive vice presidents (not members of the executive management committee)
1x	Select senior vice presidents based on job responsibility

They do this to align the interests of management and shareholders. The theory goes that you will work your butt off in the best long-term interests of the organization if you have quite a bit of your future lashed to the deck.

Believe it or not, this is a good thing. It will hurt when you tell your spouse that you are dropping six or seven figures in a stock buy of your company. But you will take a hypervigilant stance going forward. It is amazing how much more the words of a deal mean when your own money is a part of the profit/loss equation.

---

1 This is not smart. Talk to your financial advisor about investment diversity. They will already warn you about owning too much of your company's stock.

I'm only giving you a heads-up on this so you can be prepared. Plan on showing how confident you are in both you and your company's future when the time comes. Sign the forms like you were just waiting for the moment you could put so much of your future into one risk pool.[2] If you aren't ready for that, then it might be time to think about whether this is really the role for you. If it isn't a written policy, you can bet it is an unwritten rule.

---

2 You are truly exposed. Now your income and your savings are both at risk if your industry gets disrupted.

Financial Statements:
Time for a Crash Course.
You Also Need a Kyle

Not every lawyer went to business school. In fact, I bet most of the other lawyers I know didn't take a single accounting class in undergrad. If you end up in most legal jobs, you might go your whole career and never see a financial statement.

The problem, or great new frontier, depending on your point of view, is that our role has dramatically changed. It started a little over a decade ago. Well, a little further back if you consider the savings-and-loan scandals of the '80s and '90s. Enron, WorldCom, Tyco, and others followed in the early aughts. From that point on, if you had a future in corporate legal work, you needed to know how to read financial statements.

It's hard to believe now, but a lot of early in-house counsel wouldn't have been able to spot internal fraud on the company books if it was high-lighted in bright yellow marker. Let's face it, if we had a passion for credits, offsets, debits, and whatchamacallits,[1] we'd have been accountants. Beyond the need to spot fraud, how about just being able to measure the financial well-being of the company you work for and hopefully have a long-term investment in?

Well, you asked for help by buying this book, so here it is in a nut-shell. First, a financial statement isn't one document. It's a lot of different

---

1 That is an official accounting term. I'm almost sure of it.

documents. It is made up of all kinds of financial worksheets. There are balance sheets, income statements, and cash flow statements. Each one has a different purpose and tells you something about your company.

You will also often see a summary report. This is just a form that outlines the basic financial footing of the organization and shows how the company is using the money that makes up its capital. Looking at this document, you should be able to see how healthy a business is generally. Is it bleeding cash and likely to miss payroll next week? Is it flush with liquid capital and just dying for something to invest it in? All this is pretty clear from the summary report.

But the devil is in the details. It's true in litigation, and it's true in financial statements. I'll let you in on a little secret. I went to undergrad just for business. I took a ton of business math and accounting classes. I still can't read these documents as well as a person with a master's in finance and a CFA designation. I can get by. I could probably bluff my way through most situations. I can't get to the nuance of the details necessary to spot the devil or his tracks. I'm just not that good.[2]

So I did what every decent business leader does, and you should too. I found a Kyle. Every business has one. Kyle is the guy who dreams in numbers. I once asked for some random report on a cost analysis. I thought it would take ten minutes. A week later I got a 100-MB spreadsheet with eighteen tabs at the bottom and a complete breakdown of every cost variable known to man. It seems Kyle had an attention to detail and a love of the business side of math. I love Kyle.

I found my Kyle by accident. But given enough time, I'd have found him on purpose. You should start looking for yours now. You are going to need one. Find out what makes Kyle tick, and give him whatever it is. Is it praise or a seat at the table? It isn't always money. Find it, and use it to get as much of his time as you can.

You want him to help you know what you are looking at. When you review the financial statement, you want the story behind the story. Why did cash on hand change so much since the last statement? Why did earning, or specifically Earnings Before Interest and Taxes (EBIT), dip when it had been so consistent in years past? If your CFO was using EBIT as a

---

2 I'm also not that smart, no matter how smart I think I am.

measure of corporate health, why is she now referencing Earnings Before Interest, Tax, Depreciation, and Amortization (EBITDA) instead? These are all great questions. They are great questions for your Kyle.

Now let's pretend you haven't found your financial analyst or your analyst just isn't as great as my Kyle or doesn't have the time for you.[3] Now what? Well you could shell out two or three grand for a mini-MBA for corporate lawyers. You could attend an ABA TIPS in-house boot camp put on by their corporate counsel committee.[4] These are great ideas. You also should read a few intro books and financial websites to get you started. For now, here's the primer:

Let's start with the balance sheet. It's just a document that summarizes your company's assets, liabilities, and shareholders' equity at a snapshot in time. These three balance sheet segments give you a picture about what the company owns and owes. It will also show you the amount of equity owned by investors and how much is owed from borrowing. Reading this document is like reading a basic health screening from your doctor.

They call it a balance sheet because both sides of the equation better balance out. In theory, the assets on the one side must equal the equity of the owners and the liabilities on the other side. When these don't match up, you have a problem. Is someone stealing? Are inventories being improperly valued? These are things that you should be able to at least notice and ask questions about.[5]

The other form you should have a basic understanding of is an income statement. According to Investopedia, an income statement is a financial statement that reports a company's financial performance over a specific accounting period. Financial performance is assessed by giving a summary of how the business incurs its revenues and expenses through both operating and nonoperating activities. It also shows the net profit or loss incurred over a specific accounting period.

---

3 If your Kyle is like mine, everyone wants his time to analyze everything. You better be likeable. Have you tried beer?

4 Shameless plug. I'm partial.

5 This probably won't be as big an issue for those going to large publicly traded businesses. By the time you are reading a balance sheet, no fewer than a hundred hands have looked at it. Fraud will be more hidden. For those at small private companies, oh boy. Don't assume fraud, though. It might just be incompetence.

You'll see these on a 10k for every publicly traded company. It wouldn't hurt you to go online at the SEC website and check a few out. See what they look like. Why are they so important? Well, if you were looking to buy some stock, think about what you are seeing on this statement.

I told you the balance sheet was like a photograph. It's a snapshot, a picture of the finances on one day. Well, the income statement covers a much longer period, usually an entire accounting period. It will tell you a whole lot about where revenues are coming from and where operating expenses are going, and ultimately, it will drill down to a very key metric—income and earnings per share.

Earnings per share is the ultimate metric. Think about it. If you are an investor, an owner in a business, you want to know how much money you are making. How much are you earning? If the business is yours alone, it is pretty easy to see how you are doing. If it has a ton of investors, it makes it a little harder to gauge your return on investment. But by boiling it down to earnings per share (EPS), you can effectively weigh your investment in one company versus another.

Here's the rub. If EPS can swing investment decisions, it is also a key place where you need to be aware of some accounting "irregularities." So much hangs on a 10k. A bad earnings call can lead to firings at the C suite level.

The old days of long-term growth as a measure of corporate health and CEO job security are over. With that pressure on quarterly earnings statements comes incentive for "creativity" in accounting. As an in-house counsel, you'll be a key organizational control on preventing that kind of behavior.

You can't be an effective control if you aren't able to read basic financial documents. Get help if you have to. Attend some basic training classes for lawyers, even if you don't get continuing legal education (CLE) credits. Find your Kyle.

Even after you do all that, you still have to do the most important thing. You actually have to take the time to read company financial documents. You have to care enough to ask for backup reports to inform you of what it is you are seeing on the audited financials. Only then will you really know how your company is really doing. Don't be afraid to ask questions. It's much better to help your CFO than answer to the SEC or DOJ when they wonder if you were part of the problem.

A Business Plan: Aren't Those Just for Start-Ups?

Did you ever take a class where you were asked to write a business plan? I had my first experience with this in high school. There was a program called DECA, and only the coolest of nerds were allowed to participate.[1]

We competed in all kinds of crazy "distributive education" events. At first glance, it was a marketing class and club. But it turned out to be so much more. It was an introduction into running a business, selling products, and managing a workforce. All before I could drive, and at a regional competition, I got to meet the genius who came up with the Energizer Bunny. But that's beside the point.

What is the point? The business plan. If you didn't know better, you might assume that the business plan was something that college kids need to get their first investor for their tech start-up. Maybe if you went out and hung your own shingle, you'd need a business plan to get a line of credit to open your office and hire some staff, right?

If that's what you think, you're wrong. Every business needs a business plan. Even the most well-established, blue chip organization needs one.

How many organizations have you seen that seemed to have it all figured out, only to make large strategic blunders and ultimately fail miserably? I guarantee it is more than you think. As I am writing this, Sears is going down

---

1 Come to find out, nerds rule. We end up designing spaceships and electric cars, and solving all the world's problems.

the tubes.[2] It is literally selling off every property it has that is worth anything just to keep vendors comfortable shipping them product to prevent their stores from looking like a produce aisle in Khrushchev's Soviet grocery stores.

Why is Sears closing hundreds of its Kmart stores, selling off its beloved Craftsman tool brand at a steep discount, and borrowing money like there is no tomorrow? It is shortsighted to think they just hit a rough patch or couldn't compete with Target, which became hip to young kids. They lost their way.

They deviated off the path that their business plan had carefully groomed for them over decades of market changes. They used to have a core retail business. They were on their game. All of their brands fit into their core strategy and allowed for scalability and synergies. These aren't just buzzwords from business school. They are important, and they keep a business from banging into walls blindly and going off a cliff.

Sears neglected their business plan. It pursued acquisitions of nonsynergistic companies outside its area of expertise. It allowed competitors like Walmart and Target to steal market share in its own core business area—mass discount retail. It was distracted doing Merger and Acquisition (M&A) deals on real estate and financial companies. The real business plan sat in a desk drawer, its map to continued success being ignored.

This matters to you as the new in-house counsel of your organization. As the company's lawyer, you'll be privy to a host of company discussions by key management leaders. They will lay out plans for the company's future while you are sitting in their office or in the boardroom.

If you have read the business plans of your organization, you'll be well placed to keep them from doing a Sears.[3] When someone throws out a crazy idea of buying a small company in an industry that doesn't fit the plan and offers no economies of scale with your current organization, you should hit them over the head with the plan.

The plan should be one of the first things you think about when big bold moves are being proposed. Does the action meet the business goals? Does the action help with the roadmap for meeting those goals, or will it be a roadblock instead?

---

2 Sorry to all of the Sears lawyers reading this. We wish I could have used a different example. It will always be the Sears tower to me, too. :(

3 I sincerely hope that "doing a Sears" doesn't take off as a verb for business malpractice.

To Break Up with Outside Counsel or Just Date Other Outside Counsel on the Side?

There are some relationships that last forever. They are a match made in heaven. You love her; she loves you. Bonus if one of you is up for making the coffee every morning and walking the dog when it is negative brrrr degrees outside.

In my marriage, I'm the coffee maker and the dog walker, except on weekends. It works for us, so I don't complain. I'm not allowed to look around for a substitute and don't have the incentive or the desire. The relationship is just too good, so why entertain other offers?

Your relationship with your outside counsel shouldn't be like that. I hate to say it, and my outside counsel friends are probably spitting up their coffee if they are reading this,[1] but you need to occasionally see what else is out there. This isn't your wife; it's a vendor for your company, and they need to be continuously vetted for competency, results, and cost.

This is true no matter how good you think you have it. When it comes to law firms and lawyers, sometimes the grass is greener on the other side. If you don't go wiggle your toes in the lawn, you might not notice how much better it is, or could be.

I have a few firms I love working with. This isn't just business; it's a relationship. I know them. We have worked together on big issues facing

---

1 And cursing me out, too, if I know most of them.

the organizations I've worked for. I trust them. They have gotten me great results, give good counsel, and haven't overbilled me.

You might be asking why on Earth I would ever upset that kind of apple cart. Well, for starters, I have to. In some ways, this is a problem of the modern law firms' own doing. The days of lawyers staying at firms in established practice groups are over. Firm mergers, whole practice areas jumping ship, and some firms outright closing shop are the new normal.

As an in-house counsel, you now need a bench. You need alternatives, and sometimes you have to be prepared to move your business elsewhere without much notice. Even without the reasons already stated, there is the age-old issue of your chosen lawyer or firm just being plain old conflicted out. You simply can't assume that your lawyer can always be there when the need arises.

When you first start at your company, there are bound to be a host of outside firms already working on issues. There will be a business litigation firm, an employee and labor issues firm, an IP firm, an immigration firm for your global workforce needs, a tax firm, a public procurement firm, and at least a host of other firms handling every issue you can imagine.

You might find a scenario where almost everything is being done by one megafirm. Personally, I think this scenario is a terrible idea. You are not diversifying your risk that the firm pulls a Dewey & LeBoeuf, and I can't think of a single firm that is the best at antitrust litigation and also happens to have the best international corporate structuring attorney.

If you find yourself in this situation, your flirting with a new outside counsel idea needs to go from the eHarmony, take-your-time approach, and transition it to speed dating. There is just no way that one firm has the best lawyer in every area of law you need. No amount of economies of scale are making up for this problem.

There is also something to be said for jealousy. I have heard that ex-boyfriends and ex-girlfriends go up at least two points on a ten-point scale the minute someone hot starts talking to them. Well, the same can be said of outside firms.

You won't believe the level of attention your matters will get the minute your current counsel sees a press article about something your company is doing, a case it filed, or some other legal matter when they realize they aren't the attorneys working with you on it. You know what happens almost immediately? They look through every line of the article for the firm that beat them out on the work. Then they look up the specific attorney.

Your work on their desk on that other matter, it just went up two points on the scale. It became as desirable or more than the day you first hired them. They will stop rounding so hard on the billing for each call and will try to show you value. It isn't that they weren't acting in good faith already, but there is a subconscious incentive that they won't even recognize.

All this, and we haven't even gotten to the most important reason that you need to window-shop this relationship. It's just good business. You aren't just a lawyer now. You are a business advisor, and your business instincts will grow in this role. A single source supply chain is a business risk. If you were advising any other business, or even one of your internal clients that has been sourcing all of its raw materials and components from one source for years, you'd tell them that yourself.

We know that when it comes to our clients and can see it plain as day in the operations division, so why are we blind to it ourselves? Sometimes, we fall in love. We do irrational things when we are in love. We stay in bad relationships too long, sometimes long past their prime. It's human nature. If your outside counsel is doing their job,[2] you're in love with them.

You won't take this advice unless you do something proactive about it. I bet apples to donuts your company has a procurement policy. Find out what it is and hold yourself to the same standards that accounting, technology, and operations have to follow with their vendors. Too many legal teams don't do this, and they aren't reaping the business rewards of better strategic procurement.

So right now, before you get second thoughts and rush back into the arms of a comfortable companion, make a plan. Right now, walk down the hall to the procurement team and ask how they could help you make sure you are getting the best from your outside firms.

Go prepared with a list of lawyers you trust, things you look for, things you objectively want out of a firm. How many hours do you allow for responses to e-mails? What is an acceptable amount of work done by junior associates? Is office location important? Make a list of the lawyers you know in each area who you trust as a person and as a friend, or be honest with yourself if you haven't even researched it.

Walk into their office now and make a plan to build a deep bench of legal sources. You owe it to your client and your team.

---

2 This isn't just about their work product. They are building a relationship with you that will just plain suck you in.

"Yes Men" Need Not Apply

It didn't take long after Asiana Flight 214 crash-landed onto San Francisco Airport's tarmac for a whole host of news organizations to run with the theory that a cultural unwillingness to challenge one's elders was to blame for the crash. After all, it was a sunny, warm, clear day. There were no storms or wind. No Boeing 777 had been in a fatal crash like this before, so mechanical theories were thought to be far-fetched.

But the theory of too much respect for elders rears its head often when an Asian airliner goes down by human error, so this would be no exception. Malcolm Gladwell's research for his writing on the *Ethnic Theory of Plane Crashes* was soon being talked about ad nauseam on every network and cable news network.[1]

The theory gains traction because it makes sense, intuitively. If a culture is such that someone who is younger and not in a position of power is never supposed to question authority, how are they ever going to speak up when they think their superior is about to slam the plane on the ground? I have my doubts about this in plane crash scenarios, since no matter how much deference I give my elders, it stops at letting them accidentally kill me.

---

1 Especially CNN. They love a good plane crash story. Who can forget the BREAKING NEWS on MH Flight 370? Every ten minutes: "Breaking news, they still haven't found it, but some guy built a cool toy plane for us to kill network time with."

It really makes sense to me in non-life-threatening issues. You see it all the time. People don't speak up when their boss, mom, dad, or anyone else in authority says to do something. They might think, *Well that's a hell of a dumb move,* but they don't speak up. Why?

This isn't limited to Asian cultures, even if the people of those countries are generally more polite, culturally. This is a problem in all walks of life and it is a matter of degrees. Some people are followers and never question authority. Some people are leaders who set their own path, but even they sometimes don't speak up, depending on just how much social pressure the situation is bearing down.

That creates a problem if you are the one in authority. You are expecting to make a decision, and what do you do if no one has the guts to tell you that you are being an idiot? Just a bunch of bobble heads shaking their noggins up and down with big grins on their useless faces. Not helpful. Not at all.

But this isn't just a "them" problem. If you suck as a boss, it is a "you" problem that might be causing the bobble heads to brainlessly agree with you. How do they know they should speak their mind if you bite their heads off when they walk in the door with an opinion you don't like?

I learned a lesson like this once. We had a legal issue arise, and it hit me in the gut. It was like an MMA fighter punched me with everything she had. One minute, the new year was starting off to be completely awesome. The next thing I know, I'm in a meeting and someone basically tells me he almost violated a regulation that comes with some pretty serious penalties and would give us a big hulking black eye.

The thing is, this guy didn't know what he had done. He was just finding ways to sell and trying new things. This was one of those regulations that doesn't have a real ethical bent to it, so if you aren't a lawyer, you probably wouldn't have a clue that the action was even regulated.[2] But I was a

---

2 I'm sure we'll chat about this later; the difference between real crimes, the ones a kindergartener gets intuitively, and ones that the government in its infinite wisdom creates out of thin air on a daily basis. Think of the difference between killing, stealing, and bribing versus picking a flower in the park for your girlfriend. Turns out, your park is protected wetlands and you're facing five to ten years for being romantic.

lawyer, and I've grown pretty accustomed to spotting regulation violations when I hear them. Even B.S. ones.

So after getting more facts, and verifying that yes, we had a problem on our hands, I took my junior associate counsel with me and we walked into my boss's office to announce that we had entered a minefield. But I also came with a solution. It amounted to a lot of training and creating an entirely new set of compliance measures. It also meant a lot of costs and a lot of explaining to senior staff that they were now being regulated in an area we had up to that point avoided.

My boss told me I was wrong, and I'm pretty sure he was thinking I was an idiot. I told him he was wrong and that he'd figure it out after he read my memo and slept on it. But whether he liked it or not, it was true.

At this point, my associate counsel had turned herself into a wall-flower. She was practically becoming one with the paint and curling into a ball in the corner as my boss and I disagreed quite vocally over my under-standing of the law. I told him he'd get over it and agree with me and to call me when he did. I opened his door, grabbed my associate counsel, and walked out.

She was scared out of her mind that we would both be fired. I was pretty sure he'd come around and realize I was a genius, and the world's smartest lawyer. He came around in less than twenty-four hours. I'm still waiting on his admission that I was and am the world's smartest lawyer.

So what else came of this, besides reinforcing the idea that people should stop doubting me the first time? Well, it was a great learning opportunity for my associate. I walked into her office after our meeting with the GC and told her if she ever shirked up like that when she thought I was making a mistake, I'd fire her.

I wouldn't fire her for being wrong. I wouldn't fire her for making mistakes or making a judgment call I don't agree with. But I would fire her the minute she ever uttered anything close to, "I thought that was a bad idea."

Saying something like that tells me you had information or a belief that I was going to make a mistake or was wrong, and you let me do it without voicing your concern. That is a termination offense. There is no way I can forgive letting me slam the metaphorical aircraft into the ground, only to later have National Transportation Safety Board write a report that someone junior knew I was doing something wrong but was too much of a yes man to step up and say something.

So three things to take away:

1. Don't be a yes man.
2. Don't hire one either.
3. Don't be a jerk when someone disagrees with you, or you'll create one, and then it's your own damn fault.

LIFE ISN'T ONLY AT THE OFFICE

Of All the Things You Will Try to Do In-House, Pro Bono Might Be One of the Hardest

I hate to say this, but it's true. You are going to have a very hard time getting pro bono work and doing pro bono work. Don't get me wrong, if you are dying to work for free, you'll find someone to benefit. But that's not what I'm talking about. I'm talking about an ongoing, sustainable model of doing pro bono in-house.

When I was at my law firm, we did pro bono. It wasn't all the time, or a lot, but we did it. I had an amazing time representing prisoners and defending civil rights cases. I worked on cases for wrongfully convicted men, desperate to put some semblance of a life back to together. These were rewarding experiences. I was able to help those without means, and I honed my craft as a lawyer on diverse topics with unique obstacles.

Then I left the firm. And pro bono work has been difficult ever since. I've tried to set up mini-clinics, tried to set up an in-house pro bono project, and tried everything else you can imagine. It is one area that I just consider myself an absolute failure. I even worked with a large firm that does considerable business for my company to set up a program to work on their pro bono teams. It never got off the ground.

I read about other law departments in plenty of legal magazines, and they seem to be able to do it. Usually, these are very large law departments, so they must just have abundant resources to blow. I've run into every obstacle you can imagine in my quest, though, and just can't seem to get it done.

The biggest issue is the pro bono organizations themselves. Most of them just ignore you if you are in-house. I couldn't figure that out for the longest time. Why in the world wouldn't they love to get new volunteers? I mean, they wouldn't even return my calls. I would literally drop off a business card to the pro bono coordinator at certain bar organizations,[1] only to be completely and utterly blown off.

I finally got through to one coordinator who explained why she doesn't like working with in-house legal teams. Her biggest issue was the lack of a deep legal bench at most companies. A lot of organizations just don't have the legal staff that a big firm does. The secretaries aren't as experienced in legal filings, there are fewer paralegals to help the pro bono counsel, and the lack of dedicated legal investigators all make working with most in-house counsel more difficult.

The other issue with the lack of a bench was the lawyer herself. As explained by this pro bono staffer, lawyers often don't see pro bono issues all the way through. Lawyers at firms turn over or move offices or get promoted or have a bigger-paying client's trial. Well, if they are at a large firm, that isn't an issue. They get a more junior member of the firm to take the case over.

This just isn't a reality for most in-house legal departments—there just isn't a bench of other, younger, junior lawyers who can just be assigned a pro bono matter so that someone else can be relieved of it for more profitable undertakings. In fact, the in-house lawyer is likely to work the entire file by himself. He'll be the investigator and the paralegal and even his own legal secretary. A company just isn't as likely to let the lawyer borrow a ton of internal resources on something that isn't work related, and most of the work will be outside the staff's background knowledge to begin with.

The other big issue is insurance. A lot of in-house lawyers don't maintain insurance. At least, not in the lawyer, malpractice sense. We have insurance to cover business risks as executives in the organization,[2] but very few legal teams carry actual malpractice insurance. Some pro bono

---

1 There are a few bar organizations that continually seek contributions from me to serve low-income clients, but they won't call people back when someone wants to donate legal time?

2 Check this. You better make sure your company's directors and officers liability insurance policy covers the work you are doing.

organizations make it a requirement to carry malpractice insurance if you are going to do pro bono work for them or for the people needing their services. If doing free work is hard, paying out of pocket for your own insurance just to be used for the free work is harder. So, do you risk doing the work with no insurance? You will find some pro bono organizations that will cover you, but if you don't, are you willing to go naked?

Let's just say you get all of the above figured out. You get a pro bono agency to call you back. You get them to cover your insurance, and you even get your firm to let you use internal resources in your pursuit of justice. You might still have one major problem. Are you even licensed to do pro bono in the jurisdiction where you are practicing?

A lot of in-house counsel move to take their new corporate counsel role. My path took me from Miami to St. Louis to Washington, DC. Unless you are going to take a bar, or at least waive into multiple jurisdictions, provided that's an option, you might find yourself working at a company in a city and state for which you are only allowed to practice for your company. Just taking a pro bono case might run you afoul of laws against practicing without a license.[3]

These aren't absolute roadblocks, but they do make doing the pro bono work harder, and anything that makes giving away free work harder is likely to make it not happen at all. You have to really want to help people, or pro bono as an in-house counsel might just never happen. As a final word on this, I encourage you to check out www.CPBO.org. This nonprofit is trying to do great things in the pro bono space for corporate counsel. There are many folks who need our help, and doing pro bono will keep you grounded and make you a better lawyer.

---

3 This is just one reason to make sure you get barred in the place where you end up working. Trust me, if it isn't this, it will be a buddy needing DUI help or a relative of a friend who is fighting an unreasonable and threatening ex. You know it's true, so don't be lazy. Get admitted to the bar as a fully licensed lawyer. Don't stay on a limited corporate counsel bar status forever.

It's a Meat Market
and You're the Prime Rib

I feel bad for the ladies from college. As I've matured, those penny-a-pitcher ladies' nights seem less than gentlemanly.

Come to find out, being an in-house counsel at a lot of events is not unlike ladies' night. In this case, you get in free, you drink free, and the outside counsel and legal vendor types pay a fortune with the promise of access. Turns out, most legal events are a meat market, and the in-house guy is the featured item on the menu.

It doesn't actually have to be that way. You can find other venues to get great CLEs, network, grow your knowledge and skills, and not feel violated. It can be too easy to immediately think you'll only go to Association of Corporate Counsel events.

I'm not trying to dissuade you from that organization. I think they have great programs. There is only one problem. They are really only about corporate counsel. You will get a lot of great information, but it really will be only representing one plank of the platform that makes up being a well-rounded lawyer.

You will need to experiment. Stay involved in your local bar association, if that is getting you the knowledge and professional growth you crave. I personally find the American Bar Association Tort Trial and Insurance Practice section and the ABA Public Procurement Law section to be of the greatest benefit to my professional growth.

There is also value in mixing with lawyers who touch your area of practice and who aren't in-house. There is something to be gained by learning and socializing with lawyers who represent companies and with attorneys who represent plaintiffs and whistleblowers. You will learn a lot more than staying in an echo chamber of only corporate counsel.

So how do you handle it when you go to your local bar association and feel like a piece of meat? For one thing, you can't let it get to you. They are just marketing their practice, and it pays the bills. Without them trying to win you over, or think they have a chance to take your business home, there wouldn't be an event with all that great CLE.

Secondly, you have to shop around for the organization that minimizes that feeling. You might not find it at first. That's okay. Eventually you will. There will be an organization that feels like home for you and your new practice area. Don't feel bad if it isn't the organization you were involved with as an outside counsel. Go where you get what you need to grow in your role.

And that leads me to the most important point. Be ready to say no. It will feel a little crazy at first. Do you remember that great expense account you had at the firm to take out and wine-and-dine clients? Well, now you are in a position to be on the receiving end of that. Great meals, great wine, great restaurants you've always wanted to try.

You know what? Say no. This is going to sound nuts, but you really should turn them all down. Don't take the free dinners, don't drink the great wine, and don't let them spend for you to travel to a "retreat" at the lodge.

If the relationship is worth having, pay your own way. To some, this is sacrilege, but it matters. How impartial do you think the guy in IT is when Cisco sends him free stuff? Is he choosing Cisco as your network and server provider because it is the best provider for your company, or because he hopes to keep that golden goose pumping out eggs for him? You don't have to answer; I think you know.

Well, the same goes for lawyers and outside counsel. Even if you are picking the right lawyer at the right firm, it appears sleazy to have them spending lavishly on you for entertainment. Chances are, it also goes against your company's procurement and gift policies.[1] Just because you're the lawyer doesn't mean the rules don't apply to you.

---

1 If there isn't a policy, don't get excited and soak up the gifts. Ask why there isn't one.

There will come a time when your choice of an outside firm will come into question. You aren't getting results or you lose big at trial. You will want to be above reproach in the manner you chose that counsel. It certainly shouldn't be because he takes you out to nice restaurants and had you over to his house in the Hamptons. It should be because you thought he was the best to handle the case, and you should be able to remove any doubt by pointing out that for every great bourbon he poured you or bought at the bar, you've bought a round too.

You don't have to take my advice. The temptation to receive great meals and entertainment can be overwhelming. But ask yourself if they are lavishing this money and warmth on you for you or for your connection to the company. If you even have to think for a split second, you already know the answer. Just say no. You'll be happier in the long run.

TIME TO BE
CONVINCING

You Cannot Convince Someone of Something Until They Realize It Is in Their Benefit to Be Convinced

There has been a ton of ink spilled about confirmation bias and about how people are quickly entering a period where facts don't matter. Once an opinion forms, all contradictory evidence seems to fail to change someone's mind, and it sometimes has the opposite effect. This isn't just a problem for democracy and government policy. This is something that affects all of us at home with our families and ultimately in the workplace as well.

There is nothing more frustrating than presenting facts, demonstrable facts, and getting some incoherent statement back that flies in the face of your demonstrable evidence. I'll set it up for you. It's been a rough few quarters for earnings. The product your company launched to much fanfare last year has not only fallen flat on its face, but is also subject to a recall. So it is not selling, and you are having to take back and fix the ones you did sell. This product was key to the strategic plan your board instituted as a turnaround for years of anemic growth.

Your head of product development walks into a meeting with you, as the general counsel, and with the company's CEO. The CEO starts pointing out that this product was utter rubbish and demanding a plan. And you can't believe your ears when the VP of product development questions that his product line is trash. I mean, he is just filled with one bologna counternarrative after another:

- It was the marketing department's fault. They didn't advertise it right. (Actually, it was an all-out marketing bonanza. It was a *bet-the-company* marketing push, unparalleled in company history.)
- Sales weren't actually that bad. (Actually, they stunk. They were 48 percent below premarketing projects, which have been downward revised three times since.)
- What do you mean people don't want the product? A lack of sales doesn't mean that people don't want the product. (Actually, that's exactly what it means. When someone doesn't buy something you think they want or need, it means they don't want or need it.)

Every time you or the CEO present a fact that this VP doesn't want to believe, it must not be true. It's a rumor; it's wrong; it isn't a complete story. You just can't convince him that his product launch was a disaster and it's time to turn the ship. Welcome to the post-fact world. You will never convince this guy until he realizes it's in his interest to be convinced.

As the company lawyer, this one will be hard for you. For other senior staff, they can just say, "Do X because I say so." It is a horrible leadership style, and not very effective, but it can be used sometimes. As the GC, that doesn't work. You really need to convince people that a right choice of action is in their interest. You need to buy in because it is rare that you get to say, "X is the only choice since what you want to do is illegal."[1]

Usually, we are advising on a range of activities that all carry some legal and business risk. We are trying to let our internal business clients, the executive leadership team, and the board know about the law and the unintended consequences of their planned actions or inactions. And without fail, you will get one or two people who just won't be convinced. You'll write a great memo that outlines your position and potential outcomes. They will dispute the law as though it isn't what it says. They will dispute the potential outcomes, even though you have proof of legal outcomes that have happened in similar circumstances. They will even say the circumstances aren't similar, even though they are exactly the same.

---

1 Okay. If you have to say this all the time, you might be working for a criminal enterprise. It is time to move on. Like immediately. Find a different job.

Don't put your fist through a wall. It won't help. For this, you must be able to convince them they need to be convinced. You need leverage, a point of pain or future pain, and you need to pull the lever. When putting your memo together, look for the people who ended up personally in a point of pain in the companies that went down the road you are cautioning against. Also, look for the ones who personally came out smelling like roses. If they got stinking rich and got great press at the same time, that's like gold.

Now, don't put that all in your memo. You save that information. When the time comes, you pull it out. You use their corporate doppelgänger[2] as a mirror for them to see into the future. Do they want to see themselves being called smart or the ones who had a nice *Wall Street Journal* article making them look like a buffoon? Do they really want that to be them? This idiot from ACME company thought that too; look how it turned out for him. Boy, aren't they glad they're taking your advice?

Unfortunately, even this won't always work. Some people will become so wedded to a belief that no amount of counterevidence or logical persuasion will work. There is no denying that the phenomena has gotten worse. I could show you the data, but if you don't believe me already, it probably wouldn't help. In a post-fact world, you'll have to rely a lot more on emotional pleas and behavioral arguments.

It stinks, especially as a lawyer. We want to make good, rational arguments based on facts. I'm sorry, but facts are mattering less to a smaller percentage of the population. Be prepared to argue to emotions. And remember, you cannot convince someone of something until they realize it is in their benefit to be convinced.

---

2 Definition of *doppelgänger*, per Wikipedia: In fiction and folklore, a doppelgänger or doppelga(e)nger is a look-alike or double of a living person, https://en.wikipedia.org/wiki/Doppelg%C3%A4nger. Accessed December 5, 2016. Here, I'm clearly using this metaphorically.

It's Never a Good Idea Until It's Their Idea

Since we are on the subject of convincing people, we might as well face the twelve-ton gorilla in the room. Nobody likes to be told what to do. They do like to appear smart and have everyone tell them how wonderful their ideas are. Chief executive officers are especially used to being told that their ideas are great and how wonderful and beautiful they are. Not all CEOs, but a large majority, just aren't all that used to being told that they have a dumb idea or that there is a better way to get something done.

Too many people walk into a CEO's office and lose the confidence to tell them that they need to rethink a position. That's a shame, since sometimes the person running the organization needs to hear that what they are about to do is bad for business or places the organization in legal jeopardy.

So what do you do when the CEO keeps shooting down good ideas? Or for that matter, what do you do when any internal business client just won't listen? Well, you have to make them believe it is their idea. You see, your ideas are great. They hired you to come up with brilliant ideas and help them solve problems. It's just that sometimes those ideas aren't the ones they are ready to hear or act on. So, it needs to become their idea.

How do you do that? Well, it starts with paying really close attention to everything everyone says. It takes listening. Not just listening to respond, but listening to hear and remember. Take stock of everything everyone around you talks about. Parse out their thinking on everything. No matter is too small or irrelevant. These tidbits will come in handy later.

Then the hard part. After you've failed to convince them it's in their best interest to be convinced, and you are having a hard time making headway, you need to open up the file cabinet in your brain. You might have to dust off a few file folders and clear the cobwebs. You might have to go way back through every conversation you've had with this decision-maker.

Look for little pieces of relevant things this person has said for as long as you've known them. It might be that her husband took an aggressive tax position on a business deduction back in 1994 and the IRS hammered them. Now it's "her idea" not to take such aggressive positions on filings governed by regulatory bodies that have penalties that can be back imposed with interest, right?

You see the point. This isn't rocket science, but it isn't easy. It requires real listening and actually caring. Then it requires taking things someone has said in the past, often in passing or off the cuff, and turning the current issue into a similar fact pattern. Then you have to claim you got the idea for your proposal from them. It was their idea all along. People love their own ideas. They can't help themselves.

Keep in mind these really must have some kernel of "their idea." That is why it is so important to always be listening. You have to really know the people you are helping make important legal and business decisions. Listen to why they make the choices they make. Listen to why they choose a type of car and the dealership they went to for the purchase. Listen to how they choose a Christmas present and what it means to them. Listen to the thought process of every small and large decision they make. These are the keys to explaining why the good ideas you have for them are in line with the way they already reach other good ideas.

Here is the downside. You are just doing your job and trying to protect your client, the company. But hell hath no fury like someone who catches on quickly and feels like they are being manipulated. So you better be good at doing this and meaning it. Also, don't use this unless you absolutely have to. If you constantly have to resort to this, the jig is up. Ultimately, people won't trust you. They will just think you are conniving. I like to believe you are just being strategic and ultimately helping them make the right calls.

We Don't Get to Say, "I Told You So"

This one should seem pretty obvious. There will be many times you will wish you could scream, "I told you so!" at the top of your lungs.[1] You are going to be livid so many times you will lose track.

It will happen almost every day. Look forward to the day when it has happened so often you are numb, and the hollow space you feel in your soul doesn't even trigger you anymore. The more things you help with, the more issues you help solve, the more opportunities that someone might not take your advice. It's just math. Plain, simple math.

After a few years, all those years of advice on everything under the sun are going to lead to a series of moments in which people will beg you for help fixing the problem you told them would occur if they chose to ignore your advice. And that series of moments, once initiated, will never cease.

The problem is that every organization has turnover. So, even after you get one person trained, they will leave and be replaced by a new cog who will ignore your advice. The problem with the new cog is that they won't have been burned by all of the bad outcomes of ignoring you, so they will be another soul to ignore your advice and get burned. Good for job security, bad for heartburn.

---

1 You might actually be thinking, "I told you so, you dumb BLEEP." If saying "I told you so" is bad, adding an expletive at the end is worse. Don't do it. That temporary high will leave a nasty hangover in 3 . . . 2 . . . 1 . . .

I will never forget one project manager on a strategic communications team. If you presented her with a plan, she found a way to "forget" your advice 80 percent of the time. It led to constant headaches for the contract management team, the compliance team, the accounting folks and their pocket protectors—everyone. I would give her advice to get out of a jam, and a week or two later, I'd be getting her out of a bigger jam because she didn't stick to the plan.

I held my tongue as often as I could. I had to practically pull the other people affected by her refusal to take good advice off the walls. At one point, almost a year into this frustrating relationship, I couldn't take it anymore. I was hanging something in my office when someone burst in with a problem I thought we had solved already.

Now, I have to set the scene for you. I have an office hammer in my hand. You see, it isn't often that lawyers need hammers, so this isn't a big, Thor-sized hammer or even a hammer you give your daughter when she moves into her first apartment. It's a lawyer hammer for hanging wall plaques that make us look important. That's to say, it is a very tiny hammer.

Well, I become furious. It is a step too far. I just can't handle it anymore. I finally break my rule. I plan to go down there and scream, "I told you so" at the top of my lungs and let fly my feelings on fixing things that shouldn't be broken. So I storm into my friend's office and start laying in with the aforementioned, "I told you so."

Only one thing saved me from having to feel awful and apologize. You see, the whole time I was using my hands and gesturing. Only, in one hand was the world's tiniest lawyer hammer. So, luckily for me, I look like an absolute fool blowing my top and swinging a dinky hammer. It was nothing if not memorable, for both of us. It allowed her to laugh off my outburst, which was fortunate. It also allowed her to remember the next time I was trying to help guide her to the light.

For me, it was a learning moment without the pain that usually comes from learning moments. I got to laugh at my mistake, and ultimately build a bond with someone who up to that point had been driving me insane.

You know the ending, though. After another six months of no more issues, she left. She took a dream job at another great, venerable institution of high esteem. Which meant I had to deal with her replacement ignoring my advice.

While it worked out well, I often replay in my head all that could have gone wrong from that day. You see, we aren't supposed to berate people when they ignore us or choose a path we warn them will have consequences. That isn't our role. Our role is to be a steady hand and help them make decisions. And unfortunately, it is up to them to listen or not. If we are doing our jobs well, they will learn to trust us by getting good results based on our advice or getting bad results from ignoring it.

Either way, you can't replace the trust that gets built between a company's leaders and its lawyer when they see you fight on a hill knowing you could have helped them avoid the battle altogether if they had listened to you in the beginning. Don't say, "I told you so." Ask how you can help now. It's what they need, and it is what the organization needs from you.

Repeal and Replace!

I don't care if you are a Democrat or a Republican. I don't care if you love the Affordable Care Act (ACA) or think Obamacare was an Obamanation. Interestingly enough, quite a bit of survey research backs up the theory that it was really the "Obama" part of Obamacare that had half the country up in arms. They actually liked the parts in it when asked,[1] and most had a favorable view of the law itself when the name "Affordable Care Act" was used versus the nickname "Obamacare."[2]

None of that is relevant to this discussion, though. The first time that the phrase *repeal and replace* was uttered was sometime in late 2009. By early 2010 it was gaining steam as a Republican mantra.

As I sit here writing this, we are days away from a change in power that will usher in a Republican House, Senate, and White House. There is also a split in the Republican Party about how they are going handle this repeal-and-replace business.

---

1 www.pewresearch.org/fact-tank/2017/02/23/support-for-2010-health-care-law-reaches-new-high; http://kff.org/health-costs/poll-finding/kaiser-health-tracking-poll-november-2016.

2 See previous chapters. People aren't rational. They just think they are. http://fm.cnbc.com/applications/cnbc.com/resources/editorialfiles/2013/09/26/FI10863c-release%209-25-13.pdf.

They have been campaigning on this issue as a core platform for seven years. They have promised voters that if elected, on day one of the new president's term, the 115th Congress will have a bill on his desk to repeal and replace the ACA. Now, days from this historic event for half the country, we are bombarded with the message that they are ready for the repeal but are a little flummoxed with the replace part.

I'm not throwing shade[3] on Republicans. I actually think they need to fix a lot of what isn't working with the ACA and the health insurance market. What I am doing is pointing out that you can't claim the sky is falling, that the world is ending, that communists and pinkos are taking over health care, and that death panels are aiming at grannies across America, and then trip over your own feet when you get the chance to fix it.

What on Earth does this have to do with your role as a corporate counsel? I'm glad you asked. There will be things in your company, decisions made, and policies enacted that you will claim are wrong for your organization. You might give all kinds of sky-is-falling, worst-case scenarios to everyone on the management committee.

One day, you will get an e-mail that indicates someone is finally listening. On that day, don't be the dog that chases the car, finally catches it, and has no idea what to do and ends up getting run over. Have a plan. You should never, ever be running around screaming about how awful something is without an alternative that you think is the best legal and business avenue.

---

3 Yep. Sure did. I used a word designed for freshmen in college. I'm not sure I used it right, but I did it anyway.

YOU'RE NEVER TOO
OLD TO GROW UP

One of the Hardest Things Might Just Be a Year Without a Crisis

This might sound absurd. Why on Earth would you want to have a crisis? It is one of the great mysteries of the universe . . . at least my universe. There is this weird spot on the continuum of life where we find equilibrium. We are not bored; we are not overstressed. We are in our happy place.

This place for me, and for many lawyers, I believe, is when we have a sufficient amount of highly engaging work to feel needed and fulfilled and yet not so much work as to feel like we are drowning. That is the spot where all is well.

My father-in-law has retired three times. He's not a lawyer, but I think his experience is instructive to my point. When I was first dating his daughter, he was retired from active duty in the US Army, working for the highway patrol, and he was a curmudgeon of a man. He grunted at me and made his displeasure with my very existence pretty well known through body language alone. But he was otherwise happy, healthy, and had a real sense of purpose.

One day, he took off his Missouri Highway Patrol uniform and retired, again. If you know people who can't sit still without a sense of purpose, you already know what happened next. That old coot went right back to work—in Uncle Sam's army. That's right, he went straight back to the military and couldn't have been happier. He needed a purpose; we were back at war, and he felt needed.

Lawyers aren't much different. When we are cranking away at a crisis for our clients, we have direction, purpose, and a sense of self-satisfaction. When things are going well, and the seas are calm, we get restless.

There is a downside to this when you go in-house. As outside counsel, it is your job to handle these crises. You find clients, nurture relationships, and play the long game. You know that one day, your client will be faced with something horrible. They will call you, and you will know what to do. When you are in-house, you are the lawyer, but you are also the client.[1] This creates an inherent conflict of interest. You need bad things to happen to really stretch your legs and feel necessary and useful. But it isn't in your company's interest to have horribly awful things happening.

At some point in your in-house career, you will have a boring year. Don't get me wrong, there will be legal work to do. In some ways, it is even telling of the great prophylactic work you are doing to protect your company. But it won't always be the high-speed, high-stakes legal work that puts you right into that sweet spot. You won't feel challenged to your max in those times of calm.

How you handle these times, not just in terms of workload management but in terms of finding a sense of worth, can mean the difference between remaining engaged and happy or sliding into a rut. What are you going to do when you have long since recovered from the sleepless, overworked, highly stimulating, and challenging stress times and there isn't a crisis visible on the horizon?

Plan on it now. Think about the other things you can do to stay challenged and help your organization. You don't want to find yourself in that rut. Challenges keep you honed like a sharp knife, and the calm times have a tendency to dull your abilities. There isn't much worse than a talented person adrift in a sea of complacency and boredom.

You might be wondering what happened to my father-in-law. We wound down the wars in Iraq and Afghanistan and he retired again. So did my mother-in-law. She got pretty bored as well, so she went back to work and was having the time of her life. She was working because she felt needed, not because she needed the money.

---

1 Think about it. You work there. Your friends work there. Your stock in your company rides on outcomes to legal problems.

Well, good old Dad missed Mom too much at home, so he begged her to re-retire and spend time with him. That lasted two weeks, and he went back to work again. One day, he'll retire again, for the fourth time. Some people just can't handle the calm. Something tells me you are probably one of those people too. Plan for the calm times. Be prepared to find your own challenges.

Some Guy Named Confucius Said That Only the Wisest and Stupidest Men Never Change—Allegedly

I'm not sure of quotes from men whose lives have long since passed. They end up on cool posters with inspirational pictures, but I always wonder if the right guy is getting the credit. If I ever want to appear really smart, I'll say something deep and just pass it off as Einstein.[1]

Whether he said it or not, it's valid. I saw old-timers at the firm who spent ungodly hours doing things the way they always had. They just never changed. Some did it because it worked, and some did it because they were stubborn.

I'll never forget my first foray into actually working in court. I was convinced to work for the Miami Public Defender's office as a Florida Bar Rule 11 attorney by one of my favorite professors. This rule allows certain law students who are far enough along in their studies to practice in court on behalf of certain clients as a student-lawyer. I was assigned B and C felonies and went to court for a crash course in real criminal law.

Under this rule, you need a supervising attorney to sponsor you and provide guidance and oversight. While the state of Florida is looking for free labor to represent its indigent alleged criminals, it still must make sure they are being properly represented. I was assigned one young trial

---

1 Joke. That's a joke. I wouldn't be that unscrupulous.

attorney for the C felonies and a guy who looked like he'd been practicing law for more than a hundred years for the B-level cases.[2]

It was exciting work. There was no experience like representing people facing prison time to teach you trial work in a hurry. But I became a little concerned about my older mentor on the first day. I was back from handling morning arraignments and had already met my new clients at the detention center.

I wanted to suppress a statement and what I considered an illegal search. I drafted a motion and worked hard on a supporting brief. I sent everything to my mentor's e-mail and waited. The next morning, I still hadn't heard anything. I had also sent updates on my clients and my schedule. Still I got nothing.

So, I went into his office and asked if everything was okay. Did he not respond to e-mails? Well, I'll just quote him:

"You mean that piece of sh** on the desk behind me? I've never even turned that damn thing on. That's why I have a secretary."

Needless to say, he didn't get the memo. I was e-mailing someone who didn't even believe in computers, much less Microsoft Outlook. But do you know what? It worked for him. He had a system, and it hadn't failed him yet, so why change. I'm not saying he was wise or stupid. I'm just saying it managed to work out.

This just isn't the case for an in-house lawyer. You have to adapt a little. The pace of business is not like the practice of law. They aren't even the same thing. While you are still a lawyer, and a professional, the way you get things done is going to look as different as water and glue.

This isn't something to be feared. Change is slow in the legal profession and extremely fast in business. That's just the way it goes. To stay relevant, you have to adapt. Most of us aren't the wisest of men. We don't get to stay the same. Let's also try not to be the stupidest.

---

2 In case you are wondering, Cs are felonies that most frat kids have done at some point. It's a stretch to believe some should even be felonies. Bs . . . that's another story. These can land you decades in the slammer. Don't commit these. They're bad. Very bad.

You Want Me to Move Where? And Do What?

For most reading this book, achieving an in-house role might have been the Holy Grail. Maybe it is what you have always wanted. For some, it might just be the spot they somehow ended up on in the funny game called Life.

Come to think about it, many people's careers are a lot like that game. You make a choice early on, and you either go the college route or not, and like a randomly shuffled deck, people end up being handed a career based on luck of the graduation draw.

Did you graduate from college right at the dot-com bust? Chances are your career prospects were a whole lot different from those for someone who graduated four years earlier or even ten years later. That's just the deck of career cards you were given.

But just like the game of Life, occasionally you land on a spot that allows you to choose another path. If you haven't played lately, I'll refresh your memory. About halfway through, you can veer off course and go to night school, allowing you to pick a better career card. This also, if my memory serves me correctly, happens once on the board for midcareer college folks too. It's right around the spot on the board you fill your car with screaming kids and buy a second house you can't afford.

Why does any of this matter? Well, for a lot of in-house counsel, the opportunity to pull the luck lever on your career happens sometime midway through your in-house gig. If you are constantly attacking new challenges, being a great internal partner and resource, and dazzling everyone with your work ethic and devotion to the bottom line, an opportunity to leave legal will pop up.

You'll be humming along, doing great work and settling into your role, and then—*BAM*—you'll get propositioned with an opportunity to leave legal and run a business unit. Now what?

This can be an anguishing decision. Much of what you decide will have to square with the reality that not every company is the same. Some have a culture of rewarding risk and personal career growth. Some have infighting over turf, and just moving horizontally can shake the tectonic plates out from under you.

There is no right or wrong answer. Ultimately, this will need to be about what drives you and what you want out of a career. Will you get another opportunity to manage operations in Southeast Asia? Do you have your feet entirely in law, or are you enjoying your growing role and knowledge in running a company? Not every lawyer is a lawyer for life, and that's okay for some people so long as they are honest about it.

Before you think that is you, though, think it all the way through. What happens if you don't get to move back into legal? You might envision this as a few years' hiatus, upon which you'll be better suited to move up to deputy GC, or even the CLO. What if the board has other plans, and this ends up permanent? Will you be okay with that or feel orphaned from your true home?

These moves have worked for a lot of in-house counsel. Sempra Energy, a large energy firm out of San Diego, has gone on record as thinking it is great for their lawyers to move around to other business units to increase their knowledge. They aren't alone. If you are lucky enough to work for one of these organizations, you might get approached to grow your career outside the legal team. When it happens, a whole new path on the Life board game might appear, right before your eyes.

Who Wants Extra Work This Saturday Working on Something You Have No Experience Doing?

I am sorry, but if your answer isn't immediately, "Me. I do," then you will have a much better home life than most lawyers but will plateau professionally at some point. It is just the cold reality that without volunteering for extra responsibilities, you often don't grow.

This can be particularly true in the corporate setting. It can get hard to find new, challenging assignments if you let yourself settle into a rut. If you start seeing yourself as the "real estate" attorney at the office or the "employment litigation" attorney, so will everyone else. They will eventually stop asking you to expand the exciting legal areas that you can assist them with.

I remember a ton of advice I got before I left for boot camp. I've forgotten even more of it. The best advice someone gave me, and the advice I've used at every job since, is to raise your hand at a volunteer opportunity before the person asking even gets past the words "I need someone to . . ." I have yet to regret following that advice, at least after the experience of doing the thing that is required is over.

It starts on the first day. It's a mind-set. *You need something? I've got this.* Pretty soon, it imbibes you with confidence in taking on new tasks. You don't have time to overthink things if you never wait until they finish the plea for help. Just say yes.

There is a temporary downside. You will find yourself stretched, both in terms of your skill and your time commitments. It will be uncomfortable, and scary, and hard, and trying. It will also be rewarding and lead to greater opportunity than you can imagine. After a while, people will come to you before going to anyone else.[1] You will gain a reputation of being trusted, being eager, and being available when others have better things to do.

I took this advice to heart after arriving at my first permanent duty station in the Coast Guard. There wasn't a job or extra duty assignment I wouldn't volunteer for. After going through the first six months of learning every system on the ship and learning the mandatory watch qualifications, it was time to grow my role.

I stood volunteer watches on the bridge learning to navigate. French translator? Sure, I'm rusty, but I'll make it work. What? You need someone new to qualify for boarding team duty and small boat crew? I'm in. Cutter rescue swimmer? Sign me up![2]

I'm not bragging. I have a point to all this. Long before I had joined up, I had taken the LSAT. My parents, in their infinite wisdom, weren't paying any more for school.[3] I never let go of the idea that I would be a lawyer after the Coast Guard, and somehow, the best commanding officer in the fleet got wind of it.[4]

It was Thanksgiving, and I was home on holiday routine with my wife and our best friends, Charlie and Aubrey. We were making our Thanksgiving meal and just enjoying our time off, when I got a phone call from the XO. He wanted to know if the captain and he had heard correctly. Was I really going to get out of the service and go to law school?

I told him he was right, that I loved the service, but it would be time to use the GI Bill and get my law degree. It turns out that all those years of stepping into every role they could have asked for paid off in spades. I got an offer I couldn't refuse. Stay in, the service would transfer me early off my ship to a land billet, and I could start law school early with a guarantee that if I kept working as hard as I had been, they would let me spend enough time away to get my JD, and they would gain an extra three years of my time.

---

1 Of course, you also have to not get taken advantage of. I'm not unaware of this.

2 As a side note, no one told me just how cold the ocean gets at some latitudes.

3 I guess spending seven years in undergrad was too *Van Wilder* for them.

4 Captain Aaron Davenport (Ret.). I'd have followed this man anywhere. If he writes a book on leadership, you better buy it.

In addition, it would mean I could use tuition assistance to fund my law school and have a full-time salary. They would have three years to talk me into staying in the service as a lawyer once I graduated. It was a win-win. The only way it even came about was that for the years leading up to that moment, I had begged for every opportunity to get extra duty assignments.

It sucked at the time. I would want to sleep, but I'd be on an extra watch. It would be my day off, but I'd need to maintain my qualifications at the pool or going to basic EMS classes. But now I have great memories of all of those experiences, and it paid for my law school.

This advice isn't just good for the military. It works in your in-house role as well. Unless you are going in as a GC, you probably are being hired as a counsel for some area of law. Don't let that define your whole career there.

I was first hired as an in-house counsel to handle US government public procurement. It was a great role, but it would have pigeon-holed me into one small area of my company's overall portfolio of work. So I did what worked so well for me before, and I took on every extra "duty assignment" I could find. Business litigation matter? I'll take it. "Why hire a new compliance officer?" I asked. "So much of the compliance role is driven by our exposure from our public procurement work. Let me have it."

The rewards aren't just in the form of increased visibility in the organization and additional job security. You get exposure to the whole organization. I literally found myself in the back of a pickup truck in a jungle in Africa because there was an opportunity to take on extra work and I jumped on it without thinking first.

This is a challenge, and one you should accept. The next time there is a legal staff meeting, and the GC starts a sentence with anything remotely sounding like an offer for something that hasn't been done before, cut her off midsentence. You'll do it.

You'll find a way, no matter how far outside your area of law it is or how outside your comfort zone. You will call in chits from friends who will help get you up to speed. You'll research on Westlaw every night until your eyes bleed. You'll fly coach for seventeen hours to the other side of the world and happily still get your "real" job done.

It will suck. It will hurt. There will be long nights, and you will feel frustratingly over your head. But you will be rewarded, not just financially and in job security, but also in growing your personal practice. You will grow as a lawyer while so many in-house counsel plateau. Never stop learning.

Corporate Relocation: To Move or Stay, That Is the Question

I grew up thinking Anheuser-Busch (AB) made the best beer on Earth. Everyone knew that Budweiser was the undisputed king of beer, and if you went off to college, copious amounts of Natty Light were in your future.[1]

I also grew up flying TWA when it still had direct flights to Paris from St. Louis. Lambert International Airport was a bustling transit hub of activity for a region that sported quite a few Fortune 500 headquarters. General Dynamics and McDonnell Douglas called the "gateway to the west" home.

Then it all fell apart. TWA was bought out by American Airlines. General Dynamics is in DC, where I call home now. McDonnell Douglas was bought by Boeing, which just moved its missile defense division headquarters to DC as well.[2] The big loss was AB. The king of beers is now Belgian, which is fitting, since at least Belgium has a monarchy.

Lest you think this is just a St. Louis problem, I intend to correct you. I was just having dinner with a friend the other day who is a lobbyist in

---

1 I once had a third-floor walk-up in Soulard. If you are from St. Louis, you know that means I spent too many hours in bars and could smell the hops brewing at the AB brewery every morning.

2 Personally, I think these companies are just following me.

DC for a big food processor.[3] After berating her for representing "Big Food" while a bunch of amazing chefs cooked real food in her kitchen, we starting talking about her corporate headquarters. It moved from a quaint but decently sized city in the Midwest, where food is actually grown, to the urban oasis of Chicago.

This all brings me to my point. Businesses relocate. They do it for a lot of reasons. Some do it because they are bought out. Some do it because they bought some other company and move to that location. Some get a new CEO, and that CEO refuses to move to the location of the current headquarters, and some chase tax-friendly environments. Some just have to move to a location that is better suited to the industry politics of the business.[4]

When that happens, staff get moved around too. They might leave IT in the old location. AB certainly left the big Budweiser brewery in St. Louis. I'm sure they claimed it was for cost reasons, but I think it was to prevent a citywide riot.[5] They might even leave some other back office operations for a while.

One group that doesn't get much of a say? That's the executive team, which includes most lawyers. At some point in your corporate legal career, this will happen to you. You will be faced with a really difficult choice. The CEO is moving to another city, and you are being offered the chance to relocate. Now what?

This offer comes in a couple of forms. One allows you to move or stay. The other allows you to move or move on. Either one requires a real decision. Staying can be good for your family. You have a life and a home in your current city. If you are like the majority of people, you are probably in a city that you already had some roots in before you even took this job. If you have kids, they are probably wedded to the idea of staying in their own school and keeping their friends.

---

3 For those unaware, these companies turn real food into processed boxed and canned salty junk you buy at the supermarket. I won't judge, since there is a ton of it in my pantry too. Hey, you gotta eat.

4 Turns out that for gun manufacturers, being located in states that enact gun safety laws isn't good for PR.

5 Not an actual riot. Just a collective hysteria at the collapse of such a symbol of all that was St. Louis.

There is just one problem, and it's a big one. Staying can also stall your career. If you have been doing your job well, you have the ear of the entire senior management. They trust you for advice, and you are a source of direction, knowledge, and comfort. If you let them all wander off to the great new office without you, you will never hold the same position you did when you all shared an office.

This isn't just a work quality and face-time issue. This is watercooler, coffee break room important. You won't do random dinners together or grab a drink after work. You won't have lunch together or even take live meetings in the same room. You won't be there for the CEO to just walk into your office because something is on her mind.

You now are on an island. They have to work to contact you. It may be just picking up a phone or typing an e-mail, but it is still work. All of the impromptu meetings will occur without you in them. You won't be able to casually talk work at happy hour. You can't crack a bottle of wine or bourbon in your office at the end of an especially hard day and just bond.[6]

Eventually, you might lose your status as a trusted advisor. Not in the most crucial of ways for you and the work you do, but in the human connective way. And that is a career staller. At that point, you will have to accept that the next promotion probably won't be yours. That might not be a bad thing.

If you didn't immediately go all in on the chance to keep growing with the company, maybe it isn't meant to be. That isn't always bad, and it doesn't mean you aren't a good lawyer. It might just mean that the place you have created for you and your family where you live now is too important when compared against climbing the ranks at work.

The time to prepare for this is now. Businesses move, a lot. Are you all in for your company, or the city you live in? Talk to your spouse or other loved ones about it. Are they going to be on board with a move if it pops up? It doesn't mean you can't change your mind, but it will help you be prepared for what, lately at least, seems like a potential inevitability. The legal department might not always be in the city you call home.

Here is the good news. This book might be in print for only a couple years and the world might change. Cars are almost driving themselves

---

6 Or whatever nondrinkers do to bond. Not that there's anything wrong with that.

now, and everyone I know can work remotely at least occasionally. None of the advice above matters if offices as we know them change to reflect a workforce where hardly anyone goes to an office.

If that really transpires, the whole exec team might not actually see each other that often anymore anyway. For all I know, maybe we won't even have a real office to go to, and we'll all be working from any city we want. In that case, forget this whole chapter. It won't matter.

Training Your New Lawyers—Better Develop a Plan

Do you remember your law firm early years? If you went to Big Law, or even most medium-sized firms, there was a pretty regimented training program. Even the small boutique litigation firm I first went to had at least a couple senior partners who undertook my training in a semistructured manner.

If you go to well-respected firm websites, they describe their training and development like this:

- Mention professional development. Talk about how the firm takes professional development seriously and wants its lawyers to achieve the highest level of success.

- Talk about how the firm manages talent. The firm will explain how they have a detailed path and plan for your success if you work for them. They will have guideposts and benchmarks for success as you progress through their ranks. They have a specific outline and will give you pro bono opportunities to try your skills out in the real world.

- The firm will talk about how much buildup knowledge their internal training team has to impart, with a list of practical training skill programs that they will put you through.

- Professional development. The firm will assign you a mentor and help you figure out your career path and help you develop as a lawyer and a professional.

Well, those of you heading in-house are in for a surprise on the lawyer training front. Most companies don't have a formal lawyer training program at all.[1] They might have company training. They'll have development training for other roles in production, operations, and maybe even accounting. Lawyers, you're on your own.

Part of me thinks this is a vestige from a time when a company hired one lawyer who was more of an outside firm manager than a true lawyer working from within the company, actually handling legal issues of fairly large substance. That lawyer would take his CLEs and that was about it for professional development.

Times have changed—dramatically. Now, most large businesses and other organizations have a healthy staff of legal talent who work almost as an in-house law firm. Unfortunately, the legal in-house training and development programs haven't really kept up.

This is going to put you into one of two boats. You are either a young lawyer[2] who needs development or you are an old lawyer[3] who will need to train young lawyers. Neither boat is great; they're more sunfish than mega yacht.

So from your earliest days in the office, you need to start thinking of professional development. This is a profession, and it requires maintaining and growing a certain skill set to remain proficient. In addition, if you have all the knowledge in the world, your new hires won't. You are responsible for them. You're not just responsible for them as people, who are looking to you for leadership, but also in the ethical rules meaning of responsible. So you owe it to them and yourself to develop an actual plan to train them.

---

1 HP is a prime example of a company who exemplifies the exception to the rule. They actually have a kickass program to train new lawyers. You can tell them I said so.

2 Or young at heart and starting a second career with a few gray hairs.

3 Fine. We'll call you distinguished so you don't get your feelings hurt.

Let's start with an idea of what professional development entails. It is essentially like Maslow's hierarchy of needs but filled in with cool lawyer stuff:

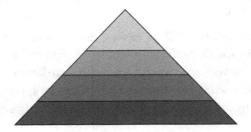

Fourth layer: This is the base. You need to be a decent lawyer. I don't mean decent, like clothed and not cursing like a sailor. I mean you should have a basic proficiency of the craft. You should write well, be well spoken, know the law, and be able to research and draft intelligently. You should have a basic understanding of how to make it through the day without committing malpractice.

Third layer: Now we are warming up. We need a level of understanding of not just the law, but also of how it applies to our company, to our industry, to our company's industries. At this level, we are able to actually know quite a bit about particular regulations that affect our industry. We can identify vulnerabilities and have a mental legal risk frame of reference for the industry.

Second layer: Now we are getting somewhere. A corporate lawyer in this zone is well versed in the law that affects her company's day-to-day operations and its industry. She doesn't stop there, though. She is following future changes in the market, with a particular eye to using the current legal framework to defend her company's beachhead from competitive challenges.

First layer: Now our hero in-house lawyer is at the pinnacle. She is looking for ways to go on the offense for her company. She is identifying ways to use the legal landscape to not just defend the company's turf, but also to attack and conquer market share. She'll see a competitor bidding on a client project that her company wants, and she will know every bit of intel on the competition and its weak spots. She will formulate plans to disqualify the competition using regulatory knowledge. She will know that there is no way their business model is in compliance with required safety standards, IT system protections required by law, or any other means of legal disqualification.

Not only that but she will be looking for ways to effect change in the legal landscape that affects her company. She will connect with other business lawyers to monitor pending legislation and rulemaking, advising her board on where and how they can apply pressure to make sure that future changes in the law benefit their business model.

The difference in skill as you make your way from new, basically trained lawyer to full-fledged legal ninja is vast. This is where the current legal training for in-house lawyers is lacking. CLE credits are as easy to come by as rain in April. It literally pours down CLE credits rain all year long if you are in-house. The bar associations don't charge most of us. The outside firms put it on for free, often even coming to your office to do it.

This is where a lot of in-house people stop learning and developing. They think that by loading up on free CLE credits on employment litigation or on business torts, they are doing their part to stay informed and trained. The problem is, they are stuck on the foundational stage of our legal Maslow pyramid.

Sure, they are doing what they need to keep their bar card, but are they really learning how to be a great in-house lawyer? Not really. They aren't even at our third-layer level. We need to figure out, as a group, how to entice our people to get above that base layer and into the layers that really make a great in-house lawyer.

This requires actually thinking proactively about professional development. Think about the skill set it takes to climb that pyramid. It takes stepping out of the traditional "legal" learning channels. We need to encourage our young in-house lawyers, and those new working from inside as well, to embrace attending business conferences about the industry. It should be required.

There is nothing wrong with developing a learning plan that takes the new lawyer through the actual operations of the business. No lawyer is above working on the factory floor or driving with the delivery guys for a few routes. Put it into the training plan. When you get into litigation over a business dispute with a client, how will you really know your side if you don't know everything about how your company makes and gets the widgets to market? The numbers, the accounting, the office staff? That is all just fluff. The rubber meets the road in production. Learn it. Formalize that learning.

Formalize the mentor program, and find new lawyers a coach. There are a lot of great coaching programs out there that will help them grow as lawyers and business associates.[4] Remember the training I mentioned earlier for operations and other departments? Put a day or two of these trainings per year onto the lawyer training schedule. They won't be legal in nature, but there is no better way to learn the business.

Every industry has issues it faces. What are the main obstacles to growth and efficient operation in your new company? Ask the others in management. Then craft a learning and development plan that finds some meeting, class, or seminar on those issues.

All of these things take time away from an in-house attorney's day job. The calls and e-mails will pile up while this learning is happening. That's okay. You need to invest in yourself, and if you are the GC or a senior counsel, you need to invest in your new talent. They can only grow so much if you only ensure they are getting the minimum CLE requirements of your local bar.

---

4 I'm partial to Gallup's strengths-based coaching models and not just because they pay my salary. It's the best model in my mind.

We All Die Sometime: Hopefully for You and Me, It Isn't Today

Nobody lives forever. That's also true for work. That gold watch in retirement doesn't come with a pension for lifelong service to the company either.

Let's face it. Everyone eventually moves on. Some people go on to do great things at other companies. Some get hit by a bus on the way to grab a bagel. This isn't a fun part of life, but it is an inevitability. Almost every other facet of life has a plus or minus percentage of variance. Will it occur? Will it not? But working at the job forever. That's an impossibility.

So if we know it is impossible, why doesn't anyone want to talk about it? Churn at a business is as inevitably destabilizing as it is inevitable in and of itself.

For one thing, no one wants to talk about their own passing. It doesn't matter if it is the "ashes to ashes" kind of passing or the passing on to a competitor. One makes us uncomfortable in a death-is-scary kind of way, and the other freaks out our bosses in a should-I-look-for-your-replacement-now sort of way.

Well, we have to talk about it. For one thing, it is recognized as poor corporate governance not to have some sort of succession plan for senior staff, at a minimum. This is easy at a publicly traded company with all independent directors. Those of you heading to small family businesses might have your work cut out convincing Jack that Jack and Sons, LLC, should have at least some succession planning.

But I'm not even talking about your role in counseling the board on all executive committee succession planning.[1] I'm talking about your successor, and if you aren't very senior, the conversations you need to have with your bosses about their plan for you in their succession line.

Trust me, this will make them just as uncomfortable as you. But this conversation must take place. For the company, it provides a smooth transition of knowledge and experience. It doesn't mean they have to stay internal, though. Part of the plan might include early retirement or separation notice followed by a period of external candidate interviews and onboarding. This would all occur prior to the current lawyer leaving.

This doesn't address our "hit by the bus" lawyer, though. Why wouldn't we also plan for any eventuality? Do a little cross training among the staff and have a plan in the event anyone, from junior associate counsel to the GC, doesn't make it in one day.

For the junior lawyer, this is especially important to get right. You are essentially trying to plan your future with the company and stake your future path to or even through your boss's job. You are also reminding them that they aren't going to be around forever, which isn't fun for them to hear.

You need to start delicately. This is sensitive. You know it and they know it. I've seen it done numerous ways, and no one way is right. I think the most effective way is to be straightforward, honest, and expect them to do the same.

Explain that you aren't leaving, you aren't trying to shake them down for money, and you aren't looking for promises they can't keep. Then lay out exactly what you want. You want to plan your future. Where does the company, and your boss particularly, see you fitting in five years from now? What about ten? If you want to be GC, say it. If you want to be the next senior litigation counsel instead, say it. Then ask if you are in the running, and if not, why?

Be ready for the answer, though. How are you going to react if they say you just don't have what the company is looking for? They will happily keep you on and see you topping out as a midgrade lawyer with a small

---

1 I'm not talking about it now, but you should know you need to do this too.

group reporting to you, but you won't rise to the top. Will you be okay with that?

There is nothing wrong with finding a role and staying in it. Not everyone needs to be the GC, and most people are actually okay with finding a good niche and living a good life doing what they love every day. But if that isn't you, and you need to grab the brass ring, you better know what to say next when or if the boss says the future is bright, but you aren't the sun.

So what if you are a GC, and a young lawyer asks about their future and you know it isn't what they think it is? The mark of a great leader is growing other great leaders.

There are a hundred reasons that your AGC might not be the right fit to succeed you. Maybe the company is going through changes that require someone with a different skill set. Maybe they are great in their role, but just aren't right to lead the legal department at your company. Either way, you owe it to them to set their expectations correctly.

Be honest. Tell them. And then fight for them. Find out what they want and help them achieve it, even if it means they end up the world's best GC at another company. Even if it means that other company is a competitor. You, and the company, are likely to get far more hurt by employing an actively disengaged lawyer whose mind is wondering about his future than if you invest in him and find him somewhere to fulfill his destiny.

This isn't a win for them and a loss for you. The whole time you are training them to land the job they really want, you and the company are getting a highly engaged, devoted attorney. This process might be short, but it might take years. Don't make the mistake of looking for their replacement and forcing them out. If they have had the guts to be honest with you, and you trust their character, invest in them and help them move on in a way that you both will be proud of.

Final Thoughts

1. Find out what software you'll have to work with. Will you have a budget to update your legal department? If you've come to a place where you cannot live without certain tools, will the team switch to your preference?

2. Will the IT team allow the software you like on the company systems? Law firms are light-years behind most companies on IT security, so don't be surprised if the stuff you like to use isn't allowed. Yep. Not my fault. I'm just the messenger. Blame the Nigerian scammers and Russian and Chinese hackers.

3. There are in-house specific software and apps that will make your life much easier. You'll have your basic legal research software. But there is a software suite made by West that I find invaluable. If you have the budget, get Practice Point. At a minimum get Practical Law.[1]

4. While we are on tools and software, you better make nice with the IT folks. If they love you, they will work late at night fixing the glitches that keep you from getting your work done. If they don't, you're stuck only getting help from the remote IT help desk. Don't get me wrong. I'm lucky. I've had great IT help desk staff. Some of you won't be so lucky. So if they want to chat with you about anything IT people are into, you better participate. Everything is online now. When tech goes bonkers, you're not working. No one

---

1 No, they didn't pay me, and they have nothing to do with the book. I did a free ad for them once because I think they're the best tool an in-house can use.

was mean to the cooks on my old Coast Guard cutter. They were the key to keeping the crew moving. Same goes for IT in corporate America.

5. A great lawyer from Akerman gave a fantastic intro at an ABA TIPS corporate counsel boot camp in Miami. I was lucky to hear him state a golden nugget I plan to tell all the lawyers transitioning in-house that I meet going forward. It's pretty straightforward but has a huge impact.

   You won't be the center of the show. At a law firm, the lawyers are the stars. We drove revenue; we won or lost the cases; we were the center of the universe at the firm. This won't be the case when you are in-house. There will be a ton of people who are the stars, and the lawyer in-house shouldn't ever be one of them.

   If you have an ego, check it at the door. You won't be the best paid or the one winning quarterly awards. Salespeople are the rain-makers of the corporate setting, and they will get the glory. Be happy for them, root them on, support them, and help them succeed. It's what pays the bills. It's why everyone is there.

6. I mentioned earlier in the book that you can't be a dream killer. That doesn't end with the lawyers. I once heard my favorite contract manager called Dream-killer Jr. by some of the sales and operations guys. Luckily, they were kidding.

   She was and is magnificent at finding solutions and getting teams to yes. But this did raise my awareness that I had to reinforce to the whole team that we would never be the No Team. We weren't where dreams go to die. We were and always would be a solutions factory.

7. You are about to learn that the expense policy is very different. I was at a great dinner the other night with about twenty-five lawyers. It ran us $125 a person. At the end of the dinner, all the outside lawyers took copies of their receipts for their expense reports. The in-house just stared at our empty wallets.

   Don't overexpense things that aren't core to the business. For one, it's just not good for the shareholders. For another thing, it will just lead to your entire travel budget getting cut. Those dinners add up.

8. While we are on expense reports, look for ways to have other people fund your expenses. Take onboard leadership positions at bar associations that are funded. Don't do it just for the bar association or the travel. Do it because it will cover your company's cost to get you great CLEs and put you in rooms with other in-house counsel whose brains you can pick for free.

   These events also happen to occur in big cities, where you will have branch offices. Use the paid travel to pop into your other offices and have face-to-face meetings with internal clients. It's on someone else's dime, and you can get a benefit for your company while growing your own brand.

9. Get to know your company's clients better than the team you support. If you have hospital chains as clients, read the *WSJ* and the local paper for every news article you can on hospitals. Put a Google alert in for every big client and industry that your company services.

   Think about all the legal and regulatory issues that are going to affect those companies and industries and provide briefings to the internal client facing teams. Let them know what their clients are going to be facing. Sometimes, the sales teams can get too focused on just what your company is delivering and forget about the bigger regulatory and legal hurdles facing the clients.

10. Final thought. Have fun. Enjoy what you are doing, not just as a lawyer but also as a business leader in your organization. You are now part of an organization that, hopefully, is building something. Be a part of it. Really dig in and try to help the company be the best at whatever it is you do.

    Even if a role has nothing to do with the law, always think about better ways to make a process work. Every time you touch a legal issue, think about all the other things going on around the periphery of the issue that you might change if it were your company. It is your company. Help make it the best.

Index

Note: n following a page number designates a footnote.